THE ONE STORY

HOLLYWOOD'S ARGUMENT FOR THE CHRISTIAN GOD

T. L. HARTLEY

WESTBOW
PRESS®
A DIVISION OF THOMAS NELSON
& ZONDERVAN

WestBow Press books may be ordered through booksellers or by contacting:

WestBow Press
A Division of Thomas Nelson & Zondervan
1663 Liberty Drive
Bloomington, IN 47403
www.westbowpress.com
844-714-3454

ISBN: 978-1-6642-7368-9 (sc)
ISBN: 978-1-6642-7369-6 (hc)
ISBN: 978-1-6642-7367-2 (e)

Library of Congress Control Number: 2022913782

Print information available on the last page.

WestBow Press rev. date: 08/16/2022

To Carol, David, Renee, Thomas, and
Levi, my greatest joys in life.

CONTENTS

ACKNOWLEDGMENTS

The ideas expressed in this book are based largely on a lecture series I attended in Nyack, New York, at the Alliance Theological Seminary. The sessions were taught by a team of Christian apologists employed by Ravi Zacharias International Ministries. I owe the greatest debt of thanks to Dr. Stuart McAllister. Without his research, dedication, and hard work, I would have no knowledge of the "One Story."

I would also like to acknowledge the help I received from my son David in the early editing of my first draft. His interest in and love of the "One Story" surpasses my own, so in many ways it was his passion that spurred me on when mine waned.

Special thanks to the skillful hands of my editor, Kathy Ide, whose professionalism and knowledge were indispensable in the completion this volume.

I am also indebted to other authors who paved the way for Dr. McAllister's study, C. S. Lewis, Joseph Campbell, and J. R. R. Tolkien, men whose names will be remembered centuries after mine is forgotten. My hope, however, is not to be remembered but only to be heard.

INTRODUCTION

I like to go to the movies, sit in the dark, and forget everything but the story unfolding before my eyes. I am not a film critic, nor do I possess the knowledge of what it takes to make a good movie, aside from a great director and lots of money. I just enjoy a good story. In the following pages, I would like to share with you a discovery I made concerning one particular story and how that discovery changed the way I see myself and understand the world around me.

All of us have favorite films, ones that we can watch over and over and that make us cry or inspire us. These movies do more than just entertain us. They touch our souls in some wonderful but inexplicable way. The majority of these films share a common theme, a single story that has been told and retold in a thousand different ways, always to the same effect.

The story that is at the heart of many of the world's most memorable books and films has been told throughout antiquity in legend and myth, in nearly every language, religion, and culture. It speaks to the hearts of both men and women. It reveals a conflict between good and evil resolved by the courage of a hero. Human beings never tire of hearing or telling this story of hope and love.

As we look at the meaning behind that story, I hope you will discover the part you are to play in this grand yet little understood epic.

PART ONE

THE POWER OF STORY

CHAPTER ONE

THE STORIES THAT TOUCH US

In the final installment of George Lucas's original Star Wars trilogy, *Return of the Jedi*, the rightful ending to the story of Luke Skywalker is told. The climactic scene of the film is a duel between Darth Vader and Luke. In this final battle, Luke fights not to kill an enemy but to save his father and his world from evil. Vader had once been Anakin Skywalker, Luke's father and a Jedi knight.

He was, over time, deceived by the emperor, blinded to his evil intent, and ultimately consumed by the dark side of the force. As the epic battle ensues, the emperor remains a spectator believing that if Vader prevails, he will continue to serve his evil purposes. If Luke prevails, he will become a younger, stronger version of what Vader had been. The emperor is convinced that he can control Luke as he had his father. He believes that Luke will turn to the dark side. For these reasons, the victor or the vanquished is of no consequence to him.

The two fight like gladiators of old, lashing at each other with their light sabers, neither able to gain a clear advantage. The whole time, the emperor is cackling in delight as he watches. As they fight, Luke tries again and again to appeal to his father, believing that some good remains in him. At the same time, Vader preaches the message of the emperor's evil, touting the power of the dark side and its inevitable triumph, urging his son to join him. Both try to turn the heart of the other as they fight, Vader on the attack and Luke retreating and defending.

Toward the end of the struggle, Luke hides in one of the dark corners of the Death Star, in the throne room of the emperor, not wishing to engage his father but to save him. In that moment, using the power of the force, Vader probes his son's mind telepathically, and though Luke tries to hide his thoughts, they are revealed to his father.

Vader then says, "Sister, a twin sister, Obi Wan was wise to hide her from me, now his failure is complete, if you will not turn to the dark side, then perhaps she will."[1]

Upon hearing these words, Luke cries out in despair, fearing for Leia, the sister he loves. He springs at Vader from his hiding place. Filled with desperation and rage, Luke is now the hunter and Vader the prey. Luke drives him back, hacking at him wildly, until Vader stumbles and falls.

Catching himself on a rail with one hand and unable to right himself, Vader can only hold out his saber to block Luke's blows. Luke stands over him and, having gained the advantage, repeatedly smashes his saber against his father's. With a final blow, Luke cuts off Vader's hand, which along with the light saber it held falls harmlessly down a deep shaft.

Vader collapses to the floor, holding up his remaining hand in submission. But Luke does not strike him. The emperor approaches, delighted with the result of the contest. He prompts Luke to kill Vader and then take his place. When Luke refuses, retracting his light saber and throwing it aside, the emperor is confused and enraged.

Raising his hands, he channels the power of the dark side into what appears to be an electrical charge that emanates from his fingers like lightning. He then directs it at the young hero. Luke falls to the ground, writhing in pain and crying out to his father for help. Vader slowly stands and assumes his place next to the emperor.

There is a brief pause in the attack and the emperor says, "Now young Jedi, you will die."[2] Mustering all his hate, he unleashes the charge a second

---

[1] *Star Wars VI, Return of the Jedi*, directed by Richard Marquand (Twentieth Century Fox, 1983, 1997, 2004).

[2] *Star Wars VI, Return of the Jedi*.

time, only this time its power is decidedly greater. Luke cries out in pain. His courage and resolve are now gone, overcome by the dark side. He is dying. As he struggles, he can only cry out to his father, who watches motionless, just behind the emperor.

The camera focuses on Vader's emotionless face, and though it is shielded with a dark mask and helmet, the conflict in his mind is palpable. At this moment, Anakin Skywalker is freed from the evil that has blinded his mind for so long. He is redeemed by his love for his son. As John William's iconic theme builds in the background, Vader becomes the hero. Seizing the emperor with his remaining hand and holding him high above his head, Vader casts him down the great shaft, leading to the core of the Death Star. And the emperor is destroyed.

Being a fan, I have watched this scene dozens of times in my home. On this particular day, I was making my usual rounds through the local Walmart. I then noticed a small group of middle-aged men watching the same scene on a television, on top of a display of DVDs. At that time, the film was over twenty years old. Yet there they stood, transfixed as the final battle between good and evil was being waged.

As I observed them from a polite distance, I couldn't help wondering what held them there. What was it that made them watch this scene one more time? The answer would come a few years later, in a series of lectures by Dr. Stuart McAllister, at a small graduate school near New York City.

My wife and I have a large library of films, and we enjoy watching our favorites again and again. Over the course of time, we became more like students of the movies than spectators. When you watch a film a dozen times, you become more aware of the details and what the director is trying to accomplish in the telling of a particular story.

My wife enjoys stories of love lost, love found, love restored, and hope in the face of life's dark realities. And she enjoys stories that speak of triumph over despair or loneliness; Disney's *Saving Mr. Banks* was one of those films. The movie tells of the difficulties that Walt Disney encountered as he attempted to transform P. L. Travers's Mary Poppins books into a film.

During the process, we are given a glimpse into Travers's childhood, including the sad story of a little girl who deeply loved her alcoholic father. Though her father adored her and she him, the difficulties of life were too much for the man to bear. He died, leaving the little girl brokenhearted and disillusioned. This story is revealed in several flashbacks throughout the film. As an adult, Pamela grew to be a bitter and difficult woman who had little use for "fun" or "fantasy." She contested nearly everything that Disney wanted to do in the film.

As the Disney writers struggled to translate the book into a movie, they inadvertently and unintentionally painted Mr. Banks to be a "villain," not knowing that the fictitious character represented Travers's beloved father. After her vehement objections, the writers reconsidered, softening the scene to which she objected and, at the same time, reworked the ending of the film so as to redeem Mr. Banks.

The change was revealed to Travers as the writers acted out the new ending, singing the song "Let's Go Fly a Kite." In the altered ending, Banks, her "father," was not portrayed as a bad or cruel man but a father who was transformed by the love of his children. It certainly was not what happened in her life but exactly what she wished would have happened. In that moment of time, her life story was rewritten and the father she adored as a little girl was redeemed, in spite of all his human flaws.

As the scene unfolded and the iconic music grew, Travers joined the performance, dancing and singing with the writers she had previously considered her enemies. Now she openly rejoiced with those same writers who had given her back the father she had lost. The scene was both profound and pointed, resulting in the tears that coursed down my face in spite of my clenched teeth and sternest efforts to resist.

My wife wept quietly but unashamedly. As we wept together in the dark, each in our own way, I thought about what I was seeing. At the same time, I thought about my wife, whose father was an alcoholic and had likewise hurt and disappointed her so long ago. In this experience, fiction touched reality, not only for Travers but for my wife and me.

Now my son has different favorites. He likes movies with heroes who face grave danger and overcome it and do noble things while venturing on great quests. As a child, my son liked books so his mother and I would read to him before he went to sleep. My wife provided a plethora of choices as collecting vintage children's books is one of her interests.

Having consumed all the standard offerings, everything from *Mike Mulligan and the Steam Shovel* to endless accounts of his favorite twosome

Frog and Toad, I decided to share with him a bigger story. One night, I introduced him to *The Hobbit,* and story time took on an entirely different feeling.

Uncharacteristically, at the age of five or six, my son would say, "Let's go to bed and read." Up to this point, reading to David was something my wife and I shared. When I began reading Tolkien's tale of a place called Middle Earth, my wife graciously stepped aside, gifting me with a magical time I would share with my son for years. It was a more wonderful gift than I have never received.

The Hobbit took some time to read, but David hung on every word. The bedtime sessions started with just fifteen or twenty minutes but quickly grew to as much as an hour or more. Sometimes, David would insist that I go on. But more often, it was of my own doing that we continued to read far past his bedtime.

Regardless of who was responsible, we both delighted in Tolkien's wonderful tale and were sad when it came to an end. When it was finished, I proposed *The Lord of the Rings,* a decidedly darker tale that Tolkien referred to as "a fairy tale for adults." This proved to be a considerable task but never a drudgery or an obligation. We would take turns reading, the process took a few years, and by the end, both of us barely fit in my son's twin bed. During this time, my wife and I introduced David to *Star Wars.* The story seized my son's fertile imagination, as it had mine decades earlier, giving us yet one more interest to share as father and son.

My personal taste in films has changed over the years, reflecting the influence of both my wife and my son. My favorite movies have always been ones that inspire hope, where good triumphs over evil, love triumphs over loneliness, and they all live happily ever after.

Long before the invention of moving pictures, stories were passed from generation to generation orally and in print. The greatest communicators of today and antiquity used stories to illustrate principles they were trying to teach or propagate. Aesop enlisted the use of fables to convey his lessons. Jesus crafted parables to teach his ideas to those who followed him. Politicians like Abraham Lincoln, Winston Churchill, and Ronald Reagan all made use of stories to speak to the issues of their day. Entertainers like Will Rogers, Mark Twain, and Garrison Keillor used stories to amuse their audiences while making powerful statements about important political and social issues. They moralized, taught, and even did a little preaching, all through the skilled use of narrative.

Apologist Dr. Stuart McAllister observed,

> People from every culture have stories, whether it is tales of family and their history told around the kitchen table, stories of national drama repeated in cultural festivals, or the endless retelling of historic fables, human tragedies or epic longing in books or movies; we enjoy and seem to thrive on stories.[3]

My father was a good storyteller. At picnics, birthdays, and holiday gatherings, we always coaxed Dad to tell the same stories about the terrible yet funny things he and his brothers did when they were young. Though we knew most of the stories by heart, we laughed every time they were retold. There was something about Dad's facial expressions, the way he raised and lowered his voice, and even the gestures of his huge hands that captivated us. Each time he told the stories, they grew in our imaginations, eventually to the status of near legend.

As an adult, I investigated the truth of Dad's tales by talking with his brothers. They substantiated his yarns, making them all the more delightful.

I remember other stories more serious in nature, ones that challenged and changed the way I saw and understood life. When my father's older brother, Chuck, was eighty-six, he told me how he fought in the Battle of the Bulge in World War II. As he shared his experience, his eyes revealed fear, his hands trembled, and tears flowed until he could speak no more. Though I have never been in battle, his story taught me something of duty and of fear—and reminded me how little I understood of such things.

My uncle could have simply told me that he was afraid or lectured me on the meaning of duty. Instead he told me his story. And I will never forget it.

Why are stories such an effective means of communicating? What is

---

[3] Stuart McAllister, lecture, "Curiosity and Power and Pull of Stories" (Alliance Theological Seminary, January 2004).

the source of their power? And how do they speak to both our hearts and our minds at the same time?

Author Eugene Peterson once said, "We live in a narrative, we live in story ... We have a beginning and an end, we have a plot, we have characters."[4] Our lives are like stories, not only to be lived but to be told and shared with others for their benefit and ours. In turn we listen to the stories of other lives in the hope of a similar benefit.

Dr. McAllister, paraphrasing colleague Dale Fincher, observed, "Story has this profound effect on us. It can remind us of things we have forgotten and awaken our senses to things we never saw before."[5]

Whether the story is based on a real-life experience or fiction and fantasy, its power to communicate remains the same. Fictional stories can remind us of important principles or show us things we have never considered. In short, stories teach us important ideas that we might otherwise fail to understand.

Two of the most famous writers of the twentieth century studied the power and pull of story and then proceeded to give their thoughts expression in stories of their own making. C. S. Lewis and J. R. R. Tolkien were both professors at Oxford University, which was one of the few things they held in common. Author Colin Duriez observed,

> Tolkien was an old-fashioned supernaturalist, who had believed the orthodox doctrines of Christianity since childhood, while Lewis as a young Oxford atheist was, at first, staunchly opposed to idealism. Thus when Lewis met Tolkien, the two men had radically opposing worldviews.[6]

They did, however, share a common interest in fairy tales, myths, and legends, considering these types of stories to be much more than just an expression of the human imagination or mere entertainment for children;

---

[4] Eugene H. Peterson, *Subversive Spirituality* (Grand Rapids, MI: William B. Eerdmans Publishing Company, 1997), 200.
[5] Stuart McAllister, lecture, "Curiosity and Power and Pull of Stories" (Alliance Theological Seminary, January 2004).
[6] Colin Duriez, *Tolkien and C. S. Lewis: The Gift of Friendship* (Hidden Spring, an imprint of Paulist Press, 2003), 27.

they were a reflection of reality and of things we have experienced, thought, or believed. A journal or record of how we see and live life, a reflection of something deep in our subconscious that can only find expression in words of a story. A fictional tale, revealing in essence what we believe, or at the very least, what we want to believe.

Lewis struggled with the idea of the human imagination and the value of fiction or fantasy. Owen Barfield, a fellow undergraduate student, friend, and part-time adversary at Oxford's Wadham College, aided Lewis in this respect. Barfield helped Lewis to think more imaginatively, to combine his imagination with his formidable intellect. This was "slow business," according to Barfield.[7]

Tolkien, on the other hand, embraced myth with a passion, seeing it not as the opposite of logic or reason but as a means to express them both creatively. His passion was evident to all who were fortunate enough to be part of one of his classes. English author, playwright, and poet W. H. Auden recalls one such class.

> I remember a lecture I attended, delivered by Professor Tolkien. I do not remember a single word he said, but at a certain point he recited, and magnificently, a long passage of Beowulf. I was spellbound.[8]

A Canadian postgraduate who heard Tolkien lecture in those early days said,

> He came in lightly and gracefully, I always remember that, his gown flowing, his fair hair shining, and he read Beowulf aloud ... The terrors and the dangers that he recounted—how I do not know—made my hair stand on end. He read like no one else I have ever heard.[9]

Isn't that often the way? We listen spellbound to a gifted speaker, a politician, a preacher, or a professor, but with the passing of time, we forget

---

[7] Duriez, 30. (*The Chicago Manual of Style* no longer advises using "ibid.")
[8] Duriez, 32.
[9] Duriez, 32.

what they were talking about. If we remember anything, it is usually a story, illustration, or perhaps a joke. If they skillfully attached the story to a concept, we remember the point they were trying to make because we remember the story. It is the story that ceases our imaginations and ceases our minds. It is story that communicates.

While a student at Oxford University, Auden was the leader of a group of communist writers. In the course of time, Auden changed his personal and political philosophy to something more acceptable for the average Englishman. Converting to Christianity, he proceeded to use his skill with words to craft poems, limericks, ballads, sonnets, and plays in an attempt to share his newfound beliefs. In 1948, he won the Pulitzer Prize. As a forceful young communist, Auden most likely employed both passion and volume in his efforts to be heard, but time and a change of heart taught him that people respond best to stories.

Parables or fables offer tidbits of knowledge or truth, little ideas wrapped up in short stories designed to pass on an idea or a concept. The thread that links them all together is the need to communicate wisdom or knowledge from one generation to the next. While people don't like being told what to do, they do enjoy listening to stories. Hence, stories are an effective teaching tool. Stories teach us, touch us, and—if we are willing—change us.

A Greek slave named Aesop wrote stories six hundred years before Jesus was born. His fables, in which animals often spoke and displayed other human characteristics, taught lessons about life. In the story of the fox and the grapes, a lone fox comes into a clearing in the woods, where he spies a cluster of grapes hanging high above his head. He proceeds to jump to reach the grapes, but his best efforts are in vain so in disgust he gives up, even though he is still very hungry. As he walks away, he mutters to himself that "the grapes were probably sour anyway."

Today, some 2,500 years later, people still say "sour grapes" when referring to someone pretending he does not want something he cannot possess.

In another of Aesop's tales, about a race between a tortoise and a hare, we learn the lesson that "slow and steady wins the race." It is a phrase still quoted today, though the story is over two thousand years old.

Jesus's parables were very much like Aesop's fables—fictional stories created to demonstrate a point or reinforce a truth. The parable of the prodigal son tells of a rebellious young man and a wise, patient father. The story goes something like this.

One day a son came to his father and asked for his inheritance because he wanted to leave home. Though the request was socially unacceptable, the wise father gave the boy his inheritance. The young man left home, traveled to a far country, and there squandered his newfound wealth in short order. Abandoned by his friends and left to fend for himself, the young man got a job at a local farm. Making hardly enough money to buy food, he decided to return to his father's home. Upon returning, he confesses his sin to his father and asks only for a job. His father, overjoyed at a lesson well learned, forgives the son and restores him to his proper place with the family.

The word *prodigal* is still used today to refer to a child who has rebelled, learned a lesson, and come back home. The term is also used in sports when an athlete returns to a team he had previously left via free agency, so the headline reads, "Prodigal Returns!"

Even though the concept is over two thousand years old, people continue to use it in contemporary language and culture today. No one understood this better than Walt Disney. He recognized the power of story not only to entertain but also to teach and inspire. He wrote,

> Out of our years of experimenting and experience we learned one basic thing about bringing pleasure and knowledge to people of all ages and conditions, which goes to the very roots of public communication. That is this—the power of relating facts, as well as fables, in story form.[10]

In his famous essay "On Fairy Stories," Tolkien wrote, "The incarnate mind, the tongue, and the tale are in our world coeval."[11] He was making the point that fictitious stories are a relevant and viable means of conveying ideas.

When I was heading off to college, I questioned my intellectual ability

---

[10] David Smith, *The Quotable Walt Disney* (New York: Disney Enterprises, Inc., 2001), 229.
[11] Verlyn Flieger, *Tolkienon Fairy-Stories* (HarperCollins UK, 2014).

and even my value as a human being. I was not a great athlete, nor was I a scholar. No one in my family before me had ever gone to college. One night, I wandered into a theater with my girlfriend to watch a movie called *Rocky*. Boxer Rocky Balboa was big and kind of dumb, and he saw himself as loser, which was how I saw myself. His triumph at the end of movie was not that he won the fight but that he didn't quit. He proved to the world, and more importantly to himself, that he was a good fighter and belonged in the ring with the best.

The message of the film was "You can do it," and with that belief, I did. When I graduated, I probably owed the greatest debt of thanks not to my professors who taught me, nor to my parents who loved and supported me, but to a fictitious story about a boxer who would not stay down.

Author Daniel Taylor observed,

> Stories link the past, present, and future in a way that tells us where we have been (even before we were born), where we are, where we could be going … Our stories teach us that there is a place for us, that we fit.[12]

Rocky taught me that.

Fictional narrative has the power not only to teach and touch but even change how we view reality. How often are our views on such things as love, loyalty, courage, and hope altered by the stories we read in books or see in movies? We strive to live like our heroes, mimicking not only their words but also their behavior. We wish we could be as noble, strong, and good as they are. Many times their example changes how we react in a given situation, make a decision, meet a crisis, or respond to a loss, in some instances making us stronger or better people in some measurable way.

Lewis and Tolkien were convinced that fiction, myth, and fairy tales were more than just imaginative expressions of the human mind. They believed that such stories were an effective means of communicating reality and truth—not just for children but for adults as well. These beliefs gave birth to *The Chronicles of Narnia*, *The Hobbit*, and *The Lord of the*

---

[12] Daniel Taylor, *The Healing Power of Stories: Creating Yourself through the Stories of Your Life* (Dublin: Gill & Macmillan, 1996), 140.

Rings—stories that encapsulate such far-reaching themes as friendship, courage, faith, duty, sacrifice, and love all communicated in a story.

The power of story to influence the human mind is well documented and something that most of us have experienced firsthand as we read a book, see a play, or watch a movie.

Unknown to most people, the most beloved stories of antiquity, along with the most lucrative films ever produced, reveal a common pattern or theme. At its core is a struggle between good and evil, the coming of a hero, a search for love and hope, and most importantly, a happy ending. You'll find this pattern in love stories, dramas, action-adventure films, and even comedies. It resonates with the young and the old, the rich and poor, and men and women alike. It is a story recognized by the human mind and embraced by the human heart, a story we never tire of telling or hearing. This is the "One Story," or the monomyth, an idea first attributed to Irish novelist James Joyce.

Later, a professor of literature at Sarah Lawrence College by the name of Joseph Campbell built on Joyce's work. Like Joyce, Campbell saw a distinct pattern in the most enduring and well-loved tales of all time. Though they appeared to be different, he concluded that they were really all the same. This pattern or theme is revealed in stories from nearly every culture and religion in the world and has been told and retold for thousands of years.

Variations of this basic story have stirred the hearts of countless millions of people throughout history, captivating the human imagination, inspiring the human heart, and touching the human soul. The "One Story" sets before humankind the hope of something more, something better. This hope, though seldom realized in a world with few happy endings, resides in nearly every human heart.

One of Campbell's students, George Lucas, revived Hollywood's fortunes in the late seventies by reshaping this same story in the context of modern technology. Later, Peter Jackson looked to J. R. R. Tolkien to tell the story to a generation of people who had forgotten the tale. A few years later, Marvel films brought to life the comic book heroes of my childhood telling the same tale to hundreds of millions of people starving for something or someone to hope and believe in.

For the few who don't look for a hero, for those who don't believe in "happily ever after," the "One Story" is nothing more than a fanciful wish or fairy tale. But for the majority of us who long for a hero and want to believe in a happy ending to our individual stories (our own lives), the "One Story" represents hope itself.

Laying personal opinion aside, regardless of how you understand the story or whether or not you embrace it, there is no denying that the vast majority of humankind is inexplicably drawn to it. With this in mind, the questions we will consider in this short volume are the following:

- Where did the story come from?
- What does it really mean?
- Why do we never tire of hearing it?
- Why does it matter so much to so many?

Before we entertain these questions, we must draw a distinction between what is high and what is low, which stories merely titillate the senses or manipulate our emotions and which ones challenge and ultimately benefit the mind as well as the soul.

CHAPTER TWO

LESSER STORIES

I have always enjoyed the Three Stooges as they provided a marvelous combination of lunacy, innocence, and mayhem. The twenty-minute shorts that made them famous did two things very effectively. They provided entertainment and made people laugh. As a young man, I would watch them with my brothers, laughing sometimes to the point of tears. The shorts did not inspire me or reveal anything of any real value, but that was not their purpose. The comedic shorts were created for fun and nothing more. With no disrespect to Larry, Curly, or Moe, I think it is reasonable to categorize these kinds of stories as of a "low" variety.

Another example of this kind of entertainment is one of my all-time favorite comedies *What about Bob?* Bill Murray plays the multiphobic but loveable Bob Wiley. He is referred for treatment to the highly successful psychiatrist Dr. Leo Marvin, played by Richard Dreyfuss. Through a series of frustrating mishaps, the loveable but dysfunctional Bob becomes emotionally attached to Dr. Marvin and his family. While this is fine with Mrs. Marvin and the kids, Bob's cloying neediness drives the good doctor over the edge. By the end of the film, Dr. Marvin has lost it and devises a way to get rid of the pesky Bob once and for all. Armed with a shotgun and a bag of dynamite, Dreyfuss sets out one night with the intention of blowing Bob to smithereens. As grim as all this sounds, there is a "happy ending," which you can discover on your own by downloading the film. Much to my shame, I have watched this silly movie a least a dozen times with my son laughing at the same gags over and over again. Like the Stooges, *What about Bob* is all about fun but nothing much else. And though it did contain a lesson about the human need for family, it too represents a "lower" form of storytelling.

On the other side of the spectrum, the film *42,* about the life of baseball player Jackie Robinson and his struggles to enter the all-white game of baseball, was both enlightening and inspiring. There were moments in the film when I cringed at the mindless hatred of bigotry and at the same time sympathized with Jackie's feelings of loneliness and rejection. As he was slowly embraced his teammates and then the fans, I was moved and inspired. Watching the film gave me something of lasting value, something I could keep and pass on. In the process of watching a two-hour movie, I was educated and challenged to better understand the lingering scars of the African American community. I think that it is fair to categorize this kind of story as a "higher" form of entertainment.

The King's Speech, which won an Oscar for Best Picture, would also fit into this "higher" category. Colin Firth plays a moving role as King George the VI of England, who was thrust into leadership at the beginning of the World War II. Suffering from a lifelong speech impediment, he enlists the help of a speech therapist, played by Oscar winner Geoffrey Rush, who aids him in the arduous task of correcting the malady. Helena Bonham Carter plays the king's wife who, along with the therapist, urges her husband on in his efforts to correct the problem. The film is both disturbing and endearing as the young king struggles to overcome what is a debilitating and, at times, humiliating problem. At the end of the film, he triumphs over his disability and his fear as he successfully delivers a speech to the British people in their darkest hour. Like the Jackie Robinson story, this film gave me something of value, inspiring my heart and challenging my mind.

Neal Gabler's book *Life: The Movie* first drew my attention to the difference between high stories and low ones in an intellectual sense. A noted expert on film, Mr. Gabler distinguishes between art and entertainment in an informative and thought-provoking book that recounts the development of the film industry in America. In the opening chapter, Gabler writes,

Almost from the beginning, something was wrong with America. When Mrs. Frances Trollope, a very proper English-woman and mother of the future novelist Anthony Trollope, toured the United States in 1828, she was revolted by the casual boorishness she found. "One man in the pit was seized with a violent fit of vomiting, which appeared not in the least to annoy or surprise his neighbors," she wrote of a visit to a theater in the nation's capital.

> Spitting was incessant; and not one in ten of the male part of the illustrious legislative audience sat according to the usual custom of human beings; the legs were thrown sometimes over the front of the box, sometimes over the side of it.

> In truth, most Americans didn't seem to know or care much about higher civilization. Whatever else one said about them, though visitors did praise their pragmatism, their industriousness, and democracy, the overwhelming majority were certainly not terribly cultured by European standards.[13]

Not unlike a teenager's contempt for the authority of his parents' generation, which he sees as an unreasonable restriction on his personal freedom, Americans of the early nineteenth century rebelled against the British culture that had given birth to them. After the American Revolution and the War of 1812, the colonists tended to view Britain with a certain degree of both suspicion and contempt. Rightly or wrongly, Americans perceived Europeans, and especially the English, as arrogant and pretentious, particularly when it came to the issue of culture. As a result, there existed a certain counterculture in America that took pride in being unrefined and to some degree even offensive by European standards.

In addition, Americans, unlike their European counterparts, lived in

---

[13] Neal Gabler, *Life: The Movie* (New York: Vintage Books, a Division of Random House, Inc., 1998), 11–12.

a country where finding your next meal was a bigger concern than what was playing at the local theater—if there was a local theater at all. Regular armed conflicts with Native Americans and the ever-present danger of wild animals like mountain lions, wolves, and bears commanded more time and attention than did the fine arts. America was a new country being forged in a great wilderness that presented considerable hardship, with little time or attention to devote to things like painting, music, or literature.

Lacking the orchestras and the great concert halls of Europe, Americans found other ways to entertain themselves. With limited choices and resources, early Americans turned to more basic kinds of entertainment—simpler, less refined, and more accessible to the general population. In the industrial age that followed, colleges, universities, and great concert halls were erected, and America began to produce its own great musicians, painters, and writers. But the American culture remained decidedly different from that of Europe.

Another factor pointing to the difference between art and entertainment was economic. Lines were drawn between rich and poor, the educated and those who lacked the means to be formally educated. Those with time and money enjoyed art and music in its highest forms: the symphony, the opera, and the great plays of Shakespeare. Those who could not afford such niceties looked for something else and found it in what became known as "entertainment." Financial necessity gave rise to venues like vaudeville, carnivals, and sideshows, a lesser kind of art designed for the common man and woman. It was simpler, easier, and cheaper for the one who produced it, and the same for those who consumed it. Entertainment became a lesser form of art. Gabler explains the difference.

> For the custodians of culture, art was sublime. It redirected one's vision from the sensual to the intellectual, from the temporal to the eternal, from the corporeal to the spiritual, all of which made art a matter not only of aesthetics but of morality as well, because its effect was to encourage one's better self.[14]

---

[14] Gabler, 15.

Originally, art was a human effort to create something of beauty, whether a sculpture, a symphony, or a painting. These early efforts most often were copies of something found in the real world, a representation of a human body, a landscape, a flower, or an animal. Something seen as beautiful was reproduced on canvas or in stone, while less tangible things like feelings, hopes, and dreams were expressed in the music of great symphonies and operas.

To create great works of art, one must be self-disciplined and hardworking. Developing the ability to paint a masterpiece, sculpt the magnificence of the human form in stone, or compose a symphony that would move people to tears demands both effort and intellect. For such endeavors as these, people have to strive to "better" themselves through hours of study and disciplined practice, not to mention financial sacrifice, while at the same time denying themselves things like comfort, leisure, and even rest.

Entertainment was not about bettering oneself, working hard, aspiring to high ideals, or achieving a better understanding of the world. It was just about fun. While art represented years of study, dedication, and effort, both to produce and to appreciate, entertainment could be achieved by something as simple as disrobing in a burlesque show, slipping on a banana peel, or telling a joke. Art appealed to the intellect; entertainment appealed to the senses and emotions.

In many of entertainment's early expressions, sex and violence were employed as key elements. Today's TV and film industries have raised the bar (or lowered it) to a whole new level of graphic entertainment. Video games have followed suit, providing the player with more realistic graphics and more themes that are both violent and sexual in nature. The majority of the top sellers are role-playing games that seek to create a highly detailed and sensitized experience, enabling the player to achieve actual feelings of pleasure or fear or even hatred. This, coupled with surround sound, high-definition digital images, and renewed efforts at 3D, points to the public's fascination with a kind of sensory overload designed to elicit a sensual or emotional experience that in some ways rivals reality itself, hence the term *virtual reality*. Gabler observes,

MTV testified to the fact that music alone was no longer a sufficient stimulus, high-definition and wide-screen television, virtual-reality games, and new and improved sound reproduction systems at the movies could blast you out of your seat.[15]

He goes on to say,

This is why critics in the 1990s routinely used amusement park metaphors to describe the new blockbuster films— "fun machine," "thrill ride," "joyride," "wildest movie ride," "roller-coaster ride"—until these terms became clichés. The reviewers were only expressing what the nineteenth-century critics of mass culture understood: that entertainment is basically a pleasurable form of sensory experience.[16]

Entertainment is designed to fill empty hours and empty minds with something to do that demands only a minimal effort on the part of the audience. It offers a distraction from the cares and struggles of life, a remedy to boredom or sadness, a reward for your hard work at the end of the day, a little fun.

Dutch philosopher Johan Huizinga, in a study of the play element in culture, discovered that the word *fun* was of recent origin and that no other language had an exact equivalent to the English meaning, leading him to speculate that fun was neither understood nor fully accepted until the twentieth century.[17]

In short, *fun* is an American invention, born and bred in the good old USA and exported to the world by way of modern media, first by radio, then television, and now the internet.

As therapeutic as a little fun can be, moderation is usually a good rule to follow. Much like alcohol or donuts, too much of a good thing can

---

[15] Gabler, 17–18.
[16] Gabler, 18.
[17] Gabler, 20.

create problems. Entertainment is no less addictive and no less problematic. Gabler observes,

> The etymology of "entertainment" is in all likelihood from the Latin *inter* (among) and *tenere* (to hold), Entertainment—movies, rock music, pulp novels, comic books, television, computer games—sinks its talons into us and pulls us in, holding us captive.[18]

Put more simply, the goal of most entertainment is to hold our attention, usually just long enough to glean a profit.

Consider this scenario. It's late in the evening and I'm exhausted. After dinner I retire to the couch and turn on the television. I flick through several choices and, much to my dismay, can find nothing worth watching. But for some inexplicable reason, I struggle to turn it off. I feel like I need to be entertained. I've worked hard all day and deserve a little break to help me relax before I go to bed. I find myself watching a rerun of a sitcom episode I've seen about two dozen times. I watch another and then another. Eventually I switch to a different station to watch another rerun I've seen at least a dozen times. It's now eleven o'clock and I'm more tired than I was when I sat down. To make matters worse, I've wasted about two and a half hours watching something I don't even care about. Something is holding me and won't let go. Sound familiar?

Now let's change the scenario ever so slightly and replace the television with the computer. Again I'm up too late, even though I'm so tired that I can barely sit up straight. I wander aimlessly from web site to web site, searching for something to entertain me. Even though I discover nothing that satisfies the itch, I am unable to turn it off and just go to bed. Such is the power of entertainment.

Despite the protests of nineteenth-century aristocrats, entertainment slowly but surely overtook and then overwhelmed art, because entertainment was fun. Like eating ice cream, staying up too late, and drinking too much, people seem to have a propensity to gravitate toward things that are not good for them. Entertainment was no different. In

---

[18] Gabler, 18.

time, newspaper publishers discovered they could sell more papers with sensational headlines and lurid stories of mayhem, sex, and murder than by providing the actual news. Dime store novels gave birth to romance novels, most of which were predictable, poorly written, and of questionable literary value. They were, however, entertaining, easy to write, and even easier to read, mass-produce, and distribute. Most of all, they were fun.

It was the movies, however, that ultimately outperformed and outdistanced vaudeville, carnivals, burlesque, novels, and the tabloids. Film became the perfect instrument to disseminate entertainment, in the form of stories, to the masses.

Over the next ten years, the movies took the country by storm, selling millions of tickets daily. Silent movies became "talkies," black-and-white became color, and music and special effects made the illusion complete. With the onset of the microchip and computer graphics, the most complex imaginations in literary history could find expression in a high-definition visual reality. Armed with such technological advantages, Hollywood became the home of the world's most effective and masterful storytellers.

Movies interpreted reality in a way no other art form or entertainment had, in part because they were fashioned from the materials of reality. Harvard psychology professor Hugo Munsterberg observes,

> The movies played in our heads and seemed to replicate our own consciousness. Conspiring with the dark, they seemed to cast a spell that lulled one from his own reality into theirs until the two merged.[19]

Revisiting Gabler's definition of the word *entertainment* as being something that "holds us," Gabler continued to expand on the definition, pointing to entertainment as something that not only holds us but actually draws us into ourselves. He wrote of entertainment,

> holding us captive, taking us deeper into the work itself and deeper into ourselves, or at least into our own emotions and senses, before releasing us. All one has to do

---

[19] Hugo Munsterberg, *The Photoplay: A Psychology Study* (New York: Dover Publications, 1915, 1970), 50.

is to watch people filing silently out of the movie theater, their eyes vacant, their faces slack, to see how one must reemerge after being submerged this way in film.[20]

By contrast, Gabler offers the Latin explanation for the effect that art should provide. Art was said to provide *ekstasis,* which in the Greek means "letting us stand outside of ourselves," presumably to lend us perspective. But everyone knows from personal experience that entertainment usually provides just the opposite, *inter tenere,* pulling us into ourselves to deny perspective.

The movies have taken the power of story to a whole new level. Hollywood's storytellers offer us a plethora of choices, some of a "lower" variety, the kind that pull us into ourselves, the kind designed only to entertain. At the same time, however, Hollywood also offers us stories of the "higher" variety, the kind that let us stand outside of ourselves, the kind that are more like art than entertainment, the kind of films that give us perspective and, at times, even illumination.

The "One Story" is of this decidedly higher variety offering not just to entertain us or titillate our senses but to challenge our minds and lift our hearts to a level above the mundane and commonplace. A story that lends perspective and understanding while at the same time offers a glimpse of both truth and hope.

I, like Gabler, have watched as fellow patrons exited a theater with blank faces and empty eyes. On other occasions, I have watched people leave those same theaters with broad smiles, mingled with tears, having viewed for a couple of hours one of Hollywood's many versions of Campbell's monomyth. A film of the higher variety, a story with a conflict between good and evil, a hero, and of course a happy ending.

It is this "One Story" to which we will now turn our full attention.

---

[20] Neal Gabler, *Life: The Movie: How Entertainment Conquered Reality* (New York: Vintage Books, a division of Random House, Inc., 1998), 18.

CHAPTER THREE

THE MONOMYTH

The man credited with discovering and identifying the monomyth is Joseph Campbell, a professor of literature at Sarah Lawrence College for nearly forty years. His area of expertise revolved around medieval literature, ancient myth, and legend. Campbell earned a BA from Columbia University and an MA in Arthurian studies (the King Arthur myth). In addition, he was an avid reader, noted author, and philosopher. He is best remembered for his book *A Hero with a Thousand Faces,* published in 1949.

However, it was a six-hour TV interview by journalist Bill Moyer, broadcast by PBS in 1988, followed by Moyer's book *The Power of Myth* that became the catalyst for transferring his insights and ideas from the realm of academia to the general public. The focal point of both the book and the interview was Campbell's study of the *monomyth,* a term he borrowed from Irish novelist James Joyce, who shared Campbell's interest in ancient stories and myth.

Through years of careful research, Campbell discovered that the most loved and most enduring stories of antiquity all shared a common pattern or theme, which is still evident in today's most successful and lucrative books and films. There are many variations to the "One Story," but the basic plot is always the same.

Campbell discovered it in the myths of Greece and Rome, in the stories of Hercules, Ulysses, and others. He also found it in the myths of the Nordic lands, in the tales of Odin and his sons, Thor and Loki, along with one of his favorites, Beowulf. In addition to these, he examined the Celtic myths of King Arthur and his knights of the round table, along with the myths of Africa and Asia, each time finding the same pattern. Regardless of geographical location, culture, or religion, the stories were ultimately the same.

Campbell defined the monomyth this way:

> A hero ventures forth from the world of common day into a region of supernatural wonder: fabulous forces are encountered and a decisive victory is won: the hero comes back from this mysterious journey with power to bestow boons [good things] on his fellow man.[21]

Whether we recognize it or not, we have all seen this pattern repeated thousands of times in thousands of stories.

I first encountered the monomyth in the Westerns I grew up with as a child. The plot line went something like this: Bad guys in black hats rob and terrorize a small town, placing people in danger—including a beautiful young librarian who is single and lonely. A handsome stranger rides into town on a white horse, wearing a white hat. He sets out on a perilous journey to find the villains. Though he is outnumbered and outgunned, he somehow manages to emerge victorious. He returns with good news and the stolen money, wins the librarian's heart, marries her, and lives happily ever after in a beautiful ranch just outside town.

The most astonishing part of this impressive feat is that he always managed to accomplish all this in less than sixty minutes, which included several commercials.

Now let's fast-forward to today's stories. A quick check of Wikipedia's fifty highest-grossing films reveals the same pattern. Nearly every film listed is an exact match. The few that aren't still contain several key elements of Campbell's monomyth in some distinguishable form.

These films are purchased or downloaded to be watched over and over

---

[21] Joseph Campbell, *The Hero with a Thousand Faces* (Princeton, NJ: Princeton University Press, 1949), 30.

again. Add to this the billions of dollars made in merchandising, and even the most ardent skeptic would have to admit that Campbell's story is not only fascinating to most people but has stood the test of time quite well.

For me, the most remarkable feature of this pattern is that it has remained the same over thousands of years. Untouched by the passing of time, advances in science, and ever-changing cultural norms, the story remains the same.

Walt Disney once said, "Fantasy, if it's really convincing, can't become dated, for the simple reason that it represents a flight into a dimension that lies beyond the reach of time."[22] Referring to myth as fantasy, Disney was pointing to the reality that the passing of time has no effect on a story that reaches beyond the confines of the calendar and resides not only on paper or film but in the human heart and mind as well.

Campbell would agree with Disney. He wrote, "Freud, Jung and their followers have demonstrated irrefutably that the logic, the heroes and deeds of myth survive into modern times."[23]

In *USA Today*, journalist Brian Truitt wrote a short article concerning an undated version of DC Comics Superman in October 2010. In the article, the author of the new graphic novel, J. Michael Straczynski, was quoted as saying, "Myths were never intended to become stagnant. They are interpreted and reinterpreted for every generation."[24]

Before we can begin to unpack the pieces of Campbell's definition of this single story, we must consider a glaring omission, insinuated in the definition but not stated: the conflict between good and evil. Why does the hero venture forth from the world of the common day? The obvious answer is to right a wrong. If nothing is wrong, why would you need a hero? Heroes are only needed to resolve conflict or at the very least to solve a problem. So what is the conflict? What's wrong?

Obviously there is a battle or some sort of conflict, because Campbell's definition points to the hero winning a victory over intimidating forces.

---

[22] Dave Smith, *The Quotable Walt Disney* (New York: Disney Enterprises, Inc., 2001), 248.

[23] Joseph Campbell, *A Hero with a Thousand Faces* (Princeton, NJ: Princeton University Press, 1949), 4.

[24] Brian Truitt, quoting J. Michael Straczynski in an article titled "A Look under the Hoodie of Superman," *USA Today*, October 28, 2010.

Most people, including me, would see the conflict as being between good and evil.

Perhaps this presented a philosophical problem for Campbell, because he was an intellectual atheist for whom good and evil held little meaning. For most atheists, the difference between good and evil is highly subjective and is ultimately determined by the individual. What is wrong for me may be right for you and vice versa.

Campbell didn't spend much time discussing the concepts of good or evil. Instead he concentrated on the psychological aspects of the monomyth, looking constantly to Freud for answers. Whether this omission was contrived or whether Campbell felt that the conflict between good and evil was so self-evident that it didn't need to be mentioned, I'll never know. However, identifying and understanding this conflict is imperative to our understanding of the monomyth.

In spite of the omission, all of the stories Campbell examined revealed something perceived as evil that needed to be overcome or defeated. Therefore, before we examine the role of the hero, we must identify the conflict that makes his services necessary.

Endless examples in literature and film, combined with simple deductive reasoning, point clearly to the conflict between good and evil as the starting point of Campbell's monomyth. The conflict is the reason for the hero and the story that follows. Without the empire and Darth Vader, there is no *Star Wars*. Luke Skywalker may as well have stayed on his uncle's farm.

The conflict between good and evil has been and continues to be the central theme and the driving force of the world's most memorable stories. It is something most people not only inherently understand in a cognitive sense but also feel in a psychological or emotional sense. When we watch the news and consider all the horrific things that take place in our world, we recognize evil and hope for good people to triumph over it.

In America we try to elect a hero to achieve this every four years. Unfortunately, that doesn't always work out. We long for someone or something to deliver justice and equity, but finding that hero proves to be a difficult task. I believe this is one of the reasons people gravitate to these kinds of stories.

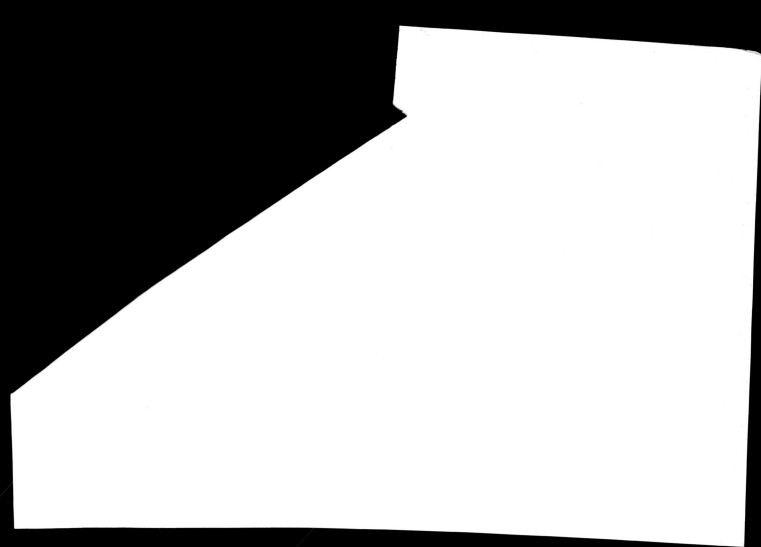

11/2022

Hi Brent—

This is the little book my pastor just got published. I think you'll enjoy it. It's easy reading and I think its quite good. I just wanted to get you a copy, so well.

So much going on here! I really need un...

As you...

...Brent.

...ee'l...

In movies where good triumphs over evil, our hope is bolstered, our convictions are vindicated, and our ideals are confirmed. Because we believe that evil should be overcome, we cheer when we see it happen on the screen. And though the stranger seated next to us in the darkened theater could be our polar opposite, they cheer right along with us because they feel the same thing we do. Why? Because something inside us feels that this is way it is supposed to be. So when good triumphs over evil, we rejoice.

In a mystery movie, evil is only revealed at the end. This holds people's attention and adds to the entertainment value of the film. However, good must triumph in the end because that is the story people most want to hear.

In the first *Star Wars* trilogy, Obi-Wan Kenobi indicates that Anakin Skywalker (Darth Vader) was destined to bring "balance" to the Force. The idea of balance is part of Buddhist philosophy, something George Lucas wanted to include in the concept of the Force. At the end of the trilogy when Darth Vader kills the emperor in defense of his son Luke, and moments later the second Death Star explodes, everybody in the theater cheers. Not because a balance between good and evil had been achieved but because evil had been defeated and good triumphed.

This same pattern can be seen in the nonfiction stories of real life, in today's news, and even in history books. While many gifted politicians, artists, musicians, and inventors are routinely forgotten or overlooked in books and film, those who were participants in the conflict between good and evil will be remembered in posterity.

Two who come to mind are Abraham Lincoln and Adolf Hitler. Both have been remembered in thousands of books, documentaries, and films. Though their stories have been told in an exhaustive sense, every visit to the local bookstore reveals yet one more volume. Lincoln is revered not only as the man who freed the slaves but also the man who saved the union and ultimately lost his life in the process. Hitler, on the other hand, is remembered as the personification of evil itself.

Evil assumes many forms in the movies. The bigger and scarier, the better. Guys like Vader, Voldemort, Sauron, and Hollywood's newest supervillain, Thanos, come to mind. There are, however, other villains who are less obvious, more commonplace, but just as imposing. Things like poverty, loneliness, racism, or self-doubt are all evils that the hero is summoned to overcome. This hero, as Campbell suggested, wears many faces, some of the most familiar found in comic books.

My mother wouldn't allow my brothers and me to buy comics books. Like other parents of the 1950s, she believed they would lead to delinquency. But my best friend, Brian, had a massive library of them. So during sleepovers on Friday nights, I got my fill.

The local barber also kept several on hand to assure the continued patronage of little boys like me. So while my two brothers got their haircuts, I feasted on superheroes of every sort.

Though I read all the books more than once, it was Superman, the son of Jor-El, who commanded my attention. My first experience with Superman, beyond the comic books of the early sixties, was the black-and-white television version of the Man of Steel, which starred George Reeves. Lots of rubber bullets and bad special effects, but I didn't care.

The seventies brought Superman to the big screen, with the promise in the trailer that "You will believe a man can fly." When John Williams's epic theme song filled the theater and Christopher Reeve took to the sky through the magic of Hollywood special effects, I soared with him. Though I did not believe a man could fly, everything in me wanted to.

Seen by many as the great American myth of the Christ, the son of Krypton assumes the role of both god and man, casting an imposing shadow on all other modern-day heroes. His primary purpose was to vanquish evil and restore that which is good.

In addition to his seemingly limitless strength, Superman possessed a moral compass that always directed him toward truth and justice. His Herculean deeds were never done for himself but always for others, for the earth's citizens, whom he was sworn to protect. He stood between the darkness of evil and the people of this world as both protector and savior.

Over my lifetime, Superman has appeared in slightly different forms, but no matter what form he took, he was always revealed in the same light: good, true, noble, and strong, the quintessential hero.

Campbell described the hero as "single-hearted, courageous and full of faith that the truth, as he finds it, shall make us free."[25] Campbell's

---

[25] Joseph Campbell, *A Hero with a Thousand Faces* (Princeton, NJ: Princeton University Press, 1949), 24.

hero was strong, self-sacrificing, and true. The moral aspect of the hero is essential to both his makeup and his purpose if he or she is to overcome evil.

Some heroes, like Batman, possess a darker side that needs to somehow be redeemed. In Marvel's first *Iron Man* movie, Tony Stark's main interests are technology, women, fast cars, and making money. Not until he is captured by terrorists and stripped of both position and power does he begin to reexamine his life. Maturing in the face of adversity in each successive movie, Tony evolves into a better man. His evolution culminates in the final scene of *The Avengers*, where he risks his life to save the world.

As the villain is fundamentally evil, the hero is inherently good.

Most heroes are not as imposing as Iron Man or Superman, and some aren't even human. In Nora Ephron's *Sleepless in Seattle*, with Tom Hanks and Meg Ryan, the unlikely hero turns out to be Hank's character's ten-year-old son, Jonah, played by Ross Malinger. Hanks portrays a loving but lonely single parent. Meg Ryan plays a woman who is outwardly happy but dissatisfied in her relationship. The evil that must be confronted is the fact that both are living void of love.

Jonah sets about to right this wrong, venturing forth from the world of common-day Seattle into a region of supernatural wonder: New York City. There he wins a decisive victory over fabulous forces, flying alone across the country, taking a cab to the Empire State building, and ultimately finding just the right woman for his lonely father.

For a hero of the four-legged variety, consider the film *Sea Biscuit*. The battle between good and evil is depicted in two ways in this film. First and most obvious is the evil we recognize as life's unfairness. The horse's owner, played by Jeff Bridges, the jockey, played by Toby Maguire, and its trainer, played by Chris Cooper, all suffer terrible misfortune in their respective lives, creating a trio of characters for which there is little hope. The second evil to overcome takes the shape of a much larger horse, War Admiral, which represents the horse-racing establishment that denounced the smaller horse as being unfit to be on the same track.

In true Hollywood fashion, Jeff Bridges actually wears a white hat the day of the big race, while the owner of War Admiral dons a black derby. The jockey's riding silks reflect the same contrast, with War Admiral's rider sporting black and gold while Maguire wears white and red.

Of course, War Admiral and his owners were not evil. But they are portrayed that way so when the race is over there is no doubt that good has triumphed. The hero of the story is the horse around whom all the main characters reconstruct their broken lives.

In the midsixties, Hollywood experimented with stories about heroes who were less moral and more conflicted. This new kind of hero was an angry, frustrated individual usually bent on revenge. The antihero was in all respects a vigilante trying to achieve a kind of "eye for an eye" justice, which mirrored the frustration of many Americans at that time. It was a difficult era in US history. John F. Kennedy had been assassinated, the country was bogged down in the Vietnam War, and oil prices and inflation were on the rise. Woodstock opened the door to the questioning of all authority, and the Water Gate scandal sadly made their point, contributing to an atmosphere of skepticism and cynicism.

Directors reflected this mindset in their project choices. Films like *China Town, Taxi Driver,* and *Death Wish* abandoned the happy ending and instead offered a dark and depressing "realism." Lacking the clear moral compass of the traditional hero, the antihero was hard to admire, dangerous to emulate, and almost impossible to love. Unlike Superman, who would achieve justice, the antihero could only accomplish revenge.

Theater profits showed marked decline as people found those movies no more encouraging than their daily newspapers.

Two movies changed this trend, bringing the hero back to the forefront of Hollywood. The first was a low-budget film about a down-and-out club fighter who, by a twist of fate, got a chance to fight for the heavyweight crown. *Rocky,* released in 1979, ushered in the return of the hero and the happy ending. And theatergoers were delighted.

Similar to other films of that day, *Rocky* was realistic—and at times a little dark and even depressing. But the story was not about a morally depraved vigilante seeking revenge. Here we had a reasonably nice guy just trying to prove himself. Rocky was certainly not Prince Charming, nor was he a pillar of virtue. But he was a hero battling not only Apollo Creed but also his own fears and self-doubt. People related to this underdog because he was likeable and fundamentally good.

However, it was not the club fighter from Philadelphia who ultimately changed Hollywood's fortunes but a little-known director's pet project that turned the tide. It was a science fiction film turned down by Universal Studios and United Artists. That film was *Star Wars*.

Like Tolkien and Campbell, George Lucas had an abiding interest in mythology, so he deliberately shaped the story to fit Campbell's monomyth. The results speak for themselves. In an interview between Bill Moyers and Joseph Campbell, which was recorded in the pages of the book *The Power of Myth*, Moyers noted that *Star Wars* came along at just the right time. He wrote,

> I think that explains in part the success of *Star Wars*. It wasn't just the production value that made that such an exciting film to watch, it was that it came along at a time when people needed to see in recognizable images the clash of good and evil. They needed to be reminded of idealism, to see a romance based on selflessness rather than selfishness.[26]

People were tired of unhappy endings, of antiheroes and dark stories that pointed only to life's miseries. *Star Wars* gave them a real hero, one they could believe in, one who spoke to their hearts. And they responded by opening their wallets.

Years later, another little-known director by the name of Peter Jackson gave expression to Tolkien's epic fantasy *The Lord of the Rings*. At the same time, Lucas offered three more *Star Wars* films: prequels of the original trilogy. Marvel Studios and DC Comics followed suit, all telling the same story, offering hero after hero and eliciting virtually the same response.

Hollywood's passing flirtation with a gritty and depressing reality and the antihero it bred crashed and burned. From the ashes rose again that hero who was virtuous and true. Only this time, instead of his trusty six-shooter, he carried a light saber, and instead of on a horse, he traveled in an X-wing fighter. His face was different, but his heart was the same. The hero was back, evil was defeated, and people cheered.

In the battle between good and evil, the hero struggles against terrible odds but ultimately achieves a decisive victory. Returning home, he brings

---

[26] Joseph Campbell, *The Power of Myth* (New York: MJF Books, 1988), 177.

with him the spoils of war to share with his community. Campbell called them "boons," good things that come as a result of his triumph. These good things can sometimes be as mundane as material possessions—perhaps returning stolen money or coming home with some great treasure to be shared.

Most often, however, the boons are far more substantial. They usually fall into two categories: justice and love.

In *Man of Steel,* Superman defeats General Zod and saves the world from an existence of dictatorial servitude, preserving the world's freedom and justice. These are "boons," good things gained in the hero's victory.

In *Sea Biscuit,* the horse saves the owner, the jockey, and the trainer by giving them a common purpose, by bolstering their confidence and by reconfirming their self-worth, not to mention restoring the joy life had stolen from them. Like Superman, *Sea Biscuit* provides a kind of justice or salvation for the downtrodden.

In *Sleepless in Seattle,* Jonah introduces his father to the perfect mate, all but guaranteeing his future happiness. Love is the boon.

Of all the boons the hero brings after his victory of vanquishing evil, none is more coveted than love. Perhaps this is why the hero almost always gets the girl.

This broadens the scope of monomyth to include stories that are not about dark lords, terrible weapons, and the end of the universe to include stories about people, life, and love, known to those of my gender as "chick flicks."

Like action-adventure films, love stories are a staple in Hollywood. Most people would see these genres as entirely different, but they don't have to be. While Hollywood works hard to craft separate films for men and for women, it always includes a little action in its love stories and a little romance in its action-adventure flicks. After all, selling two tickets is better than selling one.

Campbell's monomyth, however, can be equally manifest in either genre, for it speaks to the heart and minds of both men and women.

After *Sleepless in Seattle,* director Nora Ephron capitalized on the success of Tom Hanks and Meg Ryan's first film together and gave us *You've Got Mail.* She counted on the couple's screen chemistry to produce yet another success, and it did. The film is about the inevitability and difficulty of change. The evil to be overcome is not Fox Books but the fact that both people are in wrong relationships and therefore unhappy.

Tom Hanks is the hero, in one sense, because of his perilous quest to gain Meg Ryan's affection, which is made more difficult by fact that his company put her store out of business. The enemy he must overcome is her anger and resentment.

Ryan shares the role of hero in that she saves Hanks from repeating his father's mistakes of pursuing meaningless relationships that go nowhere. The victory is that they find each other and that they find love in a meaningful relationship.

The story is fundamentally the same. Evil is overcome, the heroes triumph, and the "boon" gained is love. The film ends as they meet in a park and the mystery of the identity of the man she learned to love online is revealed as the song "Over the Rainbow" plays gently in the background. We assume that both live happily ever after.

I would offer one final example of a love story—in this case, not romantic love but love defined in a broader sense: the love of family and friends. The holiday film *Home Alone* appears at first glance to be a story of the "lesser" variety. There is, however, far more to this Christmas tale than just the mayhem and pain inflicted on two would-be intruders by a little boy determined to protect his home. Intertwined in all the chaos of this seemingly pointless film is a wonderful love story. Penned by John Hughes, the tale is both complex and thought-provoking as it points to the human need for love and family.

The story is about Kevin and his elderly neighbor Marley, both of whom are struggling with complicated family issues. This is the evil to be overcome. Though Marley saves Kevin from Harry and Marv in the end, Kevin is the real hero, not only because of his great battle against the intruders but more importantly for suggesting that Marley reconciles with his estranged son.

The "boons" gained at the end are not only that the house is protected but that Kevin gains some much-needed reassurance from his family and learns how to better love and appreciate them. Marley's rift with his grown son is healed, and his relationship with his granddaughter is restored.

In the closing scene, after the bad guys are carted away, the boy is reunited with his family. Shortly thereafter, Mom, Dad, brother, and sister all rush off to different parts of the house to resume the chaos that is their lives. This leaves Kevin alone in the foyer. Noticing something outside, he moves slowly toward the window while John Williams's beautiful Christmas carol "Somewhere in My Memory" plays gently in the background. Across the street, he spies Marley, who is greeting his son and daughter-in-law on the sidewalk leading to his home. Scooping his granddaughter up into his arms, Marley glances toward the house and sees Kevin looking out the window. Their eyes meet. With one arm embracing his granddaughter and tears of joy coursing down his face, Marley waves the other hand to Kevin, who returns the gesture with a broad grin. Marley sets his grandchild down and, holding her hand, walks back to his house, his son and daughter-in-law following as a gentle snow falls. The hero's victory is complete, good has triumphed over evil, all that was wrong is made right, love is restored, lives and relationships are redeemed, and the ending is happy, as it should be.

This is Campbell's story: the tale of a hero bringing justice and love. But where did this amazing story come from? And why does it matter so much to so many people? And why do we tell it over and over again? There are two schools of thought, one secular and one spiritual. In the next two chapters, we will take a closer look at both.

CHAPTER FOUR

A SECULAR
EXPLANATION

The secular understanding of the "One Story" is rooted in a combination of biology and psychology. Campbell felt that the "One Story" was nothing more than an expression of the human psyche and that its origin was to be found in the human mind. He thought that the "One Story" came as a result of some sort of evolutionary process to address humankind's need for hope. He convinced himself that human beings need myths and fairy tales to comfort themselves from the harsh reality of their own mortality. To be more concise, Campbell believed that evolution made up this "One Story" to assure human survival.

He attempts to address the issue in some detail in his book *A Hero with a Thousand Faces* but ultimately offers little explanation other than evolutionary need. He based this idea on the teachings of Sigmund Freud and, to a lesser degree, Carl Gustav Jung.

Freud developed a theory of psychology based mainly on human sexuality, believing that biology alone could best explain human thought and behavior. Jung, while greatly influenced by Freud, ultimately developed a theory of psychology that moved beyond biology alone to include environmental influences. Utilizing the study of primitive man and mythology, Jung sought to explain human behavior by emphasizing the historical and cultural influences that impact human life.

Dissecting the myths he studied, Campbell sought to interpret story after story by utilizing Freudian and Jungian techniques, and for this, he was often criticized. For all his brilliance, Campbell's psychological interpretations of the monomyth were seen mostly as speculation.

In the introduction to the book *The Power of Myth*, journalist Bill Moyers points out that Campbell "was criticized for dwelling on the psychological interpretation of myth, for seeming to confine the contemporary role of myth to either an ideological or therapeutic function."[27] Moyers went on to say that he "was not competent to enter that debate, and so would leave it to others to wage."[28]

Campbell, however, had no reservations about venturing out of his area of expertise, which was literature and not psychology or psychiatry, which is why he was often criticized. Moyer went on to say, "He never seemed bothered by the controversy. He just kept on teaching, opening others to a new way of seeing."[29]

Was Campbell seeing everything clearly? Or was he seeing only what he chose to see?

All people have preconceived notions about a great many things. These notions affect the way we see and understand reality, so they can limit our ability to be objective. If my mind is already made up concerning a certain matter, it is highly likely that I will embrace only the ideas that support my view and reject any idea that challenges my position. This is typical human behavior.

As a devout intellectual atheist, Campbell grappled with a certain bias concerning God; namely, that he didn't exist. When searching for an answer as to why the "One Story" matters to people or where it came from, he was compelled to look for an answer that excluded a deity. Freud, also an atheist, provided Campbell with the ideas he needed to explain people's fascination with the "One Story," not to mention its origin.

Freudian psychology views all human thought and action as an

---

[27] Joseph Campbell and Bill Moyers, *The Power of Myth* (New York: MJF Books, Fine Communications, 1988), xx.

[28] Campbell and Moyers, xx.

[29] Campbell and Moyers, xx.

outcropping of human sexuality. If this were completely true, everything we feel, think, experience, or ponder is an expression of our sexuality. Things like love, hope, and faith become nothing more than meaningless platitudes for biological responses to certain stimuli. In a strictly biological understanding of the world, feelings, beliefs, and life itself has no purpose or meaning.

When asked if life had a purpose, Campbell responded, "I don't believe life has a purpose. Life is a lot of protoplasm with an urge to reproduce and continue in being."[30] To make his point, Campbell referenced the great German philosopher Arthur Schopenhauer, whose teachings greatly influenced both Nietzsche and Freud. Schopenhauer, in his splendid essay called "On an Apparent Intention in the Fate of the Individual," points out that when you reach an advanced age and look back over your lifetime, it can seem to have a consistent order and plan as though composed by a novelist. Events that seemed accidental and of little moment when they occurred turn out to have been indispensable factors in the composition of a consistent plot.

Schopenhauer suggests that just as your dreams are composed by an aspect of yourself of which your consciousness is unaware, so too your whole life is composed by the will within you. And just as people you meet apparently by chance become leading agents in the structuring of your life, so too will you have served unknowingly as an agent, giving meaning to the lives of others. The whole thing gears toward one big symphony, with everything unconsciously structuring everything else.[31]

For Schopenhauer, the patterns most of us recognize in our individual lives are nothing more than expressions of our own will. We come to believe what we want to believe about the purpose of our lives by linking together people and events to understand our individual stories. Fate or God are, according to Schopenhauer, is nothing more than a product of the human imagination.

Campbell believed the same argument could be used to explain the origin of the "One Story," making it just the wishful thinking of uneducated and naïve minds. The occurrences, chance meetings, conversations, and

---

[30] Campbell and Moyers, 284.
[31] Campbell and Moyers, 284.

pivotal moments in life that most people credit to some sort of fate or to the hand of God were dismissed as so much nonsense. Instead Campbell explained such things as simply expressions of the human psyche driven by sexual urges or environmental influences. He believed that life has no real meaning or purpose so the stories we tell are of little consequence, including the "One Story" that he discovered.

Seeking to temper his view, perhaps to make it a bit more palatable for the rest of us, Campbell attempted to put a positive psychological spin on his position. He wrote,

> Yet the hardness is balanced by an assurance that all that we see is but a reflex of a power that endures, untouched by the pain. Thus the tales are both pitiless and terrorless—suffused with the joy of transcendent anonymity regarding itself in all of the self-centered, battling egos that are born and die in time.[32]

Translated, we can still feel good about the fact that all these meaningless stories will continue to be told long after we are all dead.

I find no comfort in this. Purposeless and pointless expressions of the human psyche being told again and again by different people for as long as the world lasts is poor consolation for a meaningless existence. But this was all Campbell's atheistic worldview could offer.

Author Johnathan Gottschall mirrors Campbell's view when he quotes philosopher William Hirstein in his book *The Storytelling Animal*.

> The truth is depressing. We are going to die, most likely after illness; all our friends will likewise die; we are tiny insignificant dots on a tiny planet. Perhaps with the advent of broad intelligence and foresight comes the need for ... self-deception to keep depression and its consequent lethargy at bay. There needs to be a basic denial of our finitude and insignificance in the larger scene.[33]

---

[32] Joseph Campbell, *A Hero with a Thousand Faces* (Princeton, NJ: Princeton University Press, 1949), 46.

[33] Jonathan Gottschall, *The Storytelling Animal* (First Mariner Books, 2013), 175.

In other words, we need to tell ourselves that our lives have a purpose even though they don't. Our survival as a species somehow depends on an evolutionarily designed form of self-deception expressed in the story about a hero who could somehow save us from that finitude.

Again, psychology is invoked as a possible explanation as to why we humans are so fascinated with the idea of purpose and meaning for our lives and the hope such notions provide. The problem is, unlike mathematics and physics, psychology is comparatively subjective.

Certainly men like Freud and Jung have contributed greatly to our understanding of human behavior. They laid the groundwork to alleviate a considerable amount of human suffering. On the other hand, thousands of trained mental health professionals disagree with Jung and Freud, diagnosing certain problems differently and offering different remedies or therapies to address similar issues.

Psychology is a diverse and complex field of study that demands years of formal education and decades of clinical experience to master. I am not qualified to speak with any authority on complex psychological issues. But with all due respect, neither were Campbell, Gottschall, Hirstein, or any other philosopher or PhD lacking the required formal education and clinical knowledge.

In an attempt to defend his preconceived notion that God could not exist and at the same time explain the origin of the "One Story," Campbell tried to provide a naturalistic explanation for something that cannot be so explained. If, as Darwin and Freud thought, human beings are nothing more than highly evolved organisms whose only purpose is to survive and procreate, what would be the purpose of fabricating a fairy tale? How would a fairy tale contribute to our survival or our ability to propagate our genes?

Consider the shark, a creature that in my estimation far exceeds human beings in its proficiency both to survive and to procreate and has purportedly done so for millions of years. If Darwin's theories were correct in every assumption, would not the shark be the most highly and perfectly evolved of all organisms? The shark seems to have no need of fairy tales concerning such topics as hope, faith, or love. If the shark did not need such inexplicable intangibles to survive, why would humankind? The idea that nature randomly provided this complex and detailed story to keep man on top of the food chain in an evolutionary sense is highly unlikely.

For all of his brilliance, Campbell refused to consider a metaphysical explanation for the "One Story" because of his preconceived notion that God did not exist. Those who seek to better understand truth cannot hold too tightly to preconceived notions. If they hope to find the right answer, they must be willing to consider all the possibilities, however remote or contrary to their way of thinking.

Campbell, however, held to his atheistic bias. So when Bill Moyer asked why he thought all dreams come up from the psyche, Campbell replied,

> I don't know where else they would come from. They come from the imagination, don't they? The imagination is grounded in the energy of the organs of the body, and these are the same in all human beings. Since the imagination comes out of one biological ground, it is bound to produce certain themes.[34]

Trying to explain dreams, Campbell attempted to explain "imagination" (one of those distinctly human intangibles) by describing it as an energy that is somehow grounded in the organs of the body.

Campbell offers no scientific or empirical evidence to back up his theory; he simply states it as fact. Again, he falls back on the evolutionist's favorite and easiest argument, that "nature just made it happen because we needed it." The argument rings hollow and is neither conclusive nor compelling in an intellectual sense.

According to Campbell, the "One Story," as well as the human imagination that produced it, is nothing more than a manifestation of some kind of biological dictate, mysteriously and inexplicably housed in the human brain, liver, kidneys, or a combination of other organs. In attempting to explain something as complex as the human imagination in strictly biological terms, Campbell revealed the extent of his preconceived notions and his prejudice against anything spiritual or metaphysical.

---

[34] Joseph Campbell and Bill Moyers, *The Power of Myth* (New York: MJF Fine Communications, 1988), 49.

Modern atheistic authors invoke the same argument, citing genetics as the origin of the human imagination. Jonathan Gottschall wrote,

> Humans are creatures of Neverland. Neverland is our evolutionary niche, our special habitat. We are attracted to Neverland because, on the whole, it is good for us. It nourishes our imaginations; it reinforces moral behavior; it gives us safe worlds to practice in. Story is the glue of human social life, defining groups and holding them together. We live in Neverland because we can't *not* live in Neverland. Neverland is our nature. We are the storytelling animal. People dream and fantasize, our children romp and dramatize, as much as ever we are hardwired to do so.[35]

According to Gottschall, we exist in the blissful ignorance of a shared fantasy that life has meaning and purpose, until we are overtaken by the dark finality of death. I find it intriguing that atheists feel compelled to create a "story gene," a gene for the imagination, yet another gene for things like faith, love, and hope. Little genetic fixes, designed to keep us blissfully in the dark, designed to hide our eyes from the pointlessness of life and the inevitability of death.

I believe Nietzsche would have been disappointed with many of today's prominent atheistic authors and thinkers for the prefabrication of such genes. Nietzsche saw no need for fairy tales, not even ones provided by genetics. If there was anything good to be enjoyed in life, it was to be found in embracing the cold, hard facts as he saw them. Nietzsche posed the question and at the same time offered his answer when he wrote,

> What is the good? All that enhances the feeling of power, the Will to Power, and power itself in man. What is bad? All that proceeds from weakness. What is happiness? The feeling that power is increasing, that resistance has been overcome. Not contentment, but more power; not peace

---

[35] Jonathan Gottschall, *The Storytelling Animal* (First Mariner Books, 2013), 177.

at any price, but war; not virtue, but efficiency. The weak and botched shall perish: first principle of our humanity. And they ought even to be helped, to perish. What is more harmful than any vice? Practical sympathy with all the botched and weak—Christianity.[36]

Nietzsche did not court would-be followers, as do so many modern-day atheistic authors, by softening his message. His viewpoint was pure, unadulterated naturalism and his message the opposite of the "One Story." He believed that hope was for the weak-minded and that those who looked for a hero would ultimately be disappointed. He believed that life had no purpose, that love was nothing more a biological reaction, and that those who embraced such things were botched or deluded.

Only for those who taught such ideas to the weak-minded did Nietzsche hold a greater contempt: Christians. Little wonder that Adolf Hitler found Nietzsche so fascinating and that so many of his thoughts were ultimately borrowed and expressed in Hitler's writings.

Campbell embraced this same dark philosophy, but he expressed it in a less frightening and more palatable form. For all his intellectual conjecture and poetic language, the monomyth was nothing more than a literary form of sexual expression. He saw it as fictitious from beginning to end, a compilation of human fears, desires, and wishes rooted in human biology or environmental influences, nothing else.

The "One Story" became a vehicle Campbell used to support his atheistic view, dismissing the stories of religion as just more of the same nonsense. He promoted secular humanism as the ultimate good of mythology, man being both its center and its benefactor. The monomyth became to Campbell nothing more than an evolutionary placebo to provide a little comfort for humankind, numbing the pain of reality before we are all swept away into the dark abyss of death.

He finished his masterwork, *The Hero with a Thousand Faces,* by quoting Nietzsche. "Live, as though the day were here."[37] Life without

---

[36] Friedrich Nietzsche, translated by Anthony M. Ludovici, *The Antichrist* (Amherst, New York: Prometheus Books, 2000), 4.

[37] Joseph Campbell, *A Hero with a Thousand Faces* (Princeton, NJ: Princeton University Press, 1949), 391.

purpose or meaning is a depressing proposition, so Campbell suggested we do as Nietzsche did: take what we can from life and then embrace the darkness.

Campbell thought a "happy ending" was absurd because for him there could be no such thing. Instead of seeing how his discovery pointed to the possibility of something hopeful, he saw only the darkness his preconceived notions had set before him. In his intellectual confidence and atheistic bias, he dismissed the most profound and important aspects of human existence as the naïve ramblings of misguided children.

In his preoccupation with naturalism, he denied the part of himself that was the most human. Instead, like Nietzsche, he embraced nothing. So in the end, the "One Story" meant nothing to the man credited with discovering it.

CHAPTER FIVE

SPIRITUAL ILLUMINATION

As a young Oxford professor and a devout intellectual atheist, C. S. Lewis stumbled upon a quandary for which he could find no logical response. Ultimately, this quandary changed both his mind and his life.

Lewis wrote, "My argument against God was that the universe seemed so cruel and unjust. But how had I got this idea of just or unjust?"[38] In other words, how could anyone acquire a notion of what is right or wrong? Why do we think such thoughts? How is it that a simple biological organism possesses a notion of good or evil, justice or injustice, and where did it come from? Why would we care about justice in a world that the naturalist teaches us is without purpose or meaning?

The quandary of the "One Story" presents us with the same question for virtually the same reason. We care about right and wrong, we rail passionately against what we perceive as injustice, and we care about love. But where does this concern come from? And why do we persist in fashioning these concerns into stories? Some might respond that it is simply social conditioning, but that fails to explain how the same story and the same ideas find their origin in such different cultures over a span of thousands of years.

---

[38] C. S. Lewis, *The Joyful Christian* (New York: Macmillan Publishing Co. Inc., 1977), 7.

The "One Story" reveals something that most of us believe innately: good should triumph over evil, justice will ultimately be served, and love can and will be found by those who seek it. This brings us back to the questions posed earlier: Where did this story originate? And why does it matter to so many? Is this just wishful thinking, something we all want? Or is there something more here to be understood?

I believe the answer to Lewis's quandary and the meaning to the "One Story" can only be explained in a metaphysical sense. I believe it was God who made us care about such things and then fashion them into a story.

Issues of good and evil, justice and injustice, hope and love cannot be easily dismissed as optimistic or wishful thinking, for these ideas represent the core values that shape and drive human lives, whether we believe in God or not. To most humans, these are the things that matter most, our motivations for protesting or supporting political issues and donating or withholding our finances for certain causes. These are the reasons we commit to each other in marriage, volunteer for military service, and even sacrifice our lives. These are the concerns around which we shape our government and the laws of our nation. In short, the "One Story" encapsulates the greatest concerns of humankind. The Bible teaches that God caused us to be concerned about such things because we were created in His image. We care about right and wrong because God cares.

The notion of justice is central to the "One Story." That was the issue that converted C. S. Lewis from atheism to Christianity.

People intuitively distinguish good from evil. Though we may disagree on the details, we all rail against that which we see as wrong. Democrats rage against Republicans and vice versa. Environmentalists rail against industry and the NRA decries the efforts of PETA. Apologist Dr. Stuart McAllister observed,

> In conversation with any thinking person, it is easy to pick an event, an issue or a problem and quickly elicit a response. Race issues, gender issues, sexual politics, government, international affairs, etc. It does not take much time or

effort to surface a deep-seated and antagonizing concern of the heart.[39]

At the root of this concern is the shared belief that something is wrong and that justice demands that it be made right. One could argue that a sense of justice is a learned behavior, but that perspective fails to explain the origin of such ideas in the first humans. The notion that something is wrong reveals itself in the earliest stages of life, in the stories told by children.

Jonathan Gottschall discovered a pattern in the study of some 360 stories told by preschoolers. He writes,

> Children's pretend play is clearly about many things: mommies and babies, monsters and heroes, spaceships and unicorns. And it is also about only one thing: trouble. Sometimes the trouble is routine, as when, playing "house," the howling baby won't take her bottle and father can't find his good watch. But often the trouble is existential.[40]

Many of the children wrote stories about problems and evil in the world, not just in their homes or some immediate circumstance. Even children recognize that the world is not a very nice place and that something is fundamentally wrong. Like adults, children recognize evil. Though they lack the sophistication to articulate their fears, they ultimately hope for some resolution, as adults do. They look for or create a hero to come and save them, to right the wrong, to bring justice and defeat evil.

As we mature, evil becomes an enemy to be defied and ultimately defeated. But there is a problem. For all our resolve and collective intellect, the greatest evils in this world not only continue to exist but flourish. Poverty, prejudice, war, and inequity span the globe. Depression, alcoholism, drug addiction, sexual abuse, and a seemingly endless list of crimes against humankind frustrate us at every turn. Even with all the new and amazing technological advances, humankind is still unable to

---

[39] Dr. Stuart McAllister, "The Rage against Injustice and Deceit," a lecture given at Alliance Theological Seminary, Nyack, NY, 2004.
[40] Jonathan Gottschall, *The Storytelling Animal* (First Mariner Books, 2013), 33.

correct these wrongs. Nearly all our efforts to combat them are met with new and darker problems.

Aside from an occasional small victory here or there, there is little reason to be optimistic about the world or its future. Humankind seems to learn nothing from history and continues to repeat the same mistakes, committing the same crimes against both nature and one another. The Bible identifies these problems collectively as sin.

The biblical concept of sin is simple. The scriptures teach that humans should love God and care for each other as we would ourselves. The problem is we don't.

The issue of sin is not so much what we do to each other as what we fail to do. Hollywood mirrors this dilemma. Something is wrong, and what is wrong is evil, and that evil cannot be overcome by any power known to man. Whether it is Dorothy lost in the land of Oz or Luke Skywalker standing in the shadow of an evil empire, something is terribly wrong and only a hero can make it right. Consciously or subconsciously, we look for that hero, someone with the power to do what we cannot, someone big and strong enough to take on all the injustice of life.

Sadly, the best leaders the world has ever known, both men and women, ultimately fail to fix what is wrong. So we go looking for another. Hope drives us, but reality disappoints us again and again because the problem of sin in our world can't be fixed by an individual or by any system of government.

History shows our efforts to fix what is wrong to be insufficient and futile. As a result of this failure, we console ourselves by constructing stories about heroes who can solve a problem we are powerless to do anything about, heroes who can deliver both justice and the happy ending we yearn or hope for.

In Frank Darabont's 1994 film *The Shawshank Redemption*, this collective yearning is given expression in a gritty and disturbing film about prison life. The story points to the exclusively human need we all share: the need for hope. The story depicts evil, corruption, and injustice in graphic terms yet at the same time offers hope in little bits and pieces as the prisoners struggle to find some meaning in their otherwise purposeless existence.

Tim Robbins plays the part of Andy Dufresne, a man wrongfully convicted of murder. He befriends Morgan Freeman's character, Red, another prisoner serving a life term for a disproportionate crime he committed in his youth. In a fascinating tale based on the Stephen King novel, a corrupt and cruel warden played by Bob Gunton is ultimately outsmarted and brought to justice by Andy, who plays the part of the hero. In the course of these events, Andy escapes, but not before communicating an offer to Red that if he should ever be released that he should look for him in a small town on the Pacific coast of Mexico. Andy hoped to start a new life there by opening a small seaside inn and chartering fishing trips for tourists. In the course of time, Red is granted parole and released. Struggling with the adjustment of living on the "outside" and on the brink of despair, Red remembers Andy's offer. He also remembers that Andy had promised to leave him a box, hidden in a stonewall just outside of town with instructions on where to find him in Mexico.

Morgan Freeman decides to look for the box, which he finds. In it, there are a letter, money, and instructions. In the closing words of the letter, Andy writes,

> Remember Red, hope is a good thing, maybe the best of things and no good thing ever dies. I will be hoping that this letter finds you.[41]

Red buys a ticket to Mexico. As the bus careens down the road, he talks to himself.

> I hope I can make it across the border. I hope to see my friend and shake his hand. I hope the Pacific is a blue as it has been in my dreams.[42]

Then after a long pause, Red simply says, "I hope."[43] Just before the credits roll, we see Red walking alone down a long stretch of beach. At the far end of the beach, Andy is sanding the paint off an old boat. As if sensing Red's presence, he turns around and sees him. With no words spoken, he

---

[41] *The Shawshank Redemption,* directed by Frank Darabont (Warner Bros. Pictures, 1994).
[42] *The Shawshank Redemption.*
[43] *The Shawshank Redemption.*

hops down off the boat and runs to meet his friend. Red drops his suitcase and does the same. As the two men embrace, the camera pans away into the distance and the figures grow smaller as the beautiful theme, composed by Thomas Newman, fills the theater. All that is left are the sky, the sand, the ocean, and the two friends. Evil is overcome, hope is realized, and all that was wrong is made right. Viewers' smiles mingle with tears, hearts are satisfied, and minds are filled with hope.

The need for hope is singularly human. The recognition of hope realized is also an exclusively human experience. It touches those who witness it deeply and profoundly.

This film is about hope and justice. It ascribes meaning and purpose to life and demonstrates that even in dire circumstance, we can still hope. These ideas are replete in every book of the Bible, for the Bible is above all a book of hope.

In his book *Science and the Story that We Need,* author Neil Postman writes,

> In the end science does not provide the answer most of us require. Its story of our origins and our end is, to say the least, unsatisfactory. To the question "How did it all begin?," science answers, "Probably by accident." To the question "How will it all end?," science answers, "Probably by accident." And to many people, the accidental life is not worth living.[44]

If you believe in God, like I do, you are probably hoping for something more than just an accidental life. To you I offer another proposition, one that Campbell could not see: the hope of a life with purpose and meaning and a future that reaches beyond death.

Since no credible or compelling argument can be made for the "One Story's" origin being solely physical, why not consider the possibility that skeptics refuse to even ponder? What if God hardwired the "One Story" into our subconscious? What if he gave us knowledge of this story along with other intangibles like the concepts of beauty, creativity, and the

---

[44] John Eldred, *Epic* (Thomas Nelson, Inc., 2004), 9.

capacity for faith or love as clues to direct our attention back to him? What if he gave us something intangible that could not otherwise be explained—hope—in the form of a story with a happy ending to show us that there is more to life and to us than just a physical world?

J. R. R. Tolkien wrote stories revealing, as he put it, an underlying truth. A truth revealed in a story about good and evil, a hero and hope, a truth too fantastic for the mind of a hardened skeptic, a truth pointing not only to God but to heaven. Tolkien's stories, like those of George Lucas and Marvel films, along with all the stories that Campbell studied, point to the same truth, the same hope, and the same belief—namely that another world exists and it is a decidedly better world than the one in which we now live.

Skeptics see this as fantasy. Tolkien saw such tales as road markers pointing to a hidden reality, expressions of the human psyche responding to something we all feel or know inherently to be true.

Such was the case with journalist Bill Moyers, in his interview with Campbell, when he said, "These myths speak to me because they express what I know inside is true. Why is this so? Why does it seem that these stories tell me what I know inside is true?"[45] Moyer uncharacteristically repeated the question, perhaps reflecting its importance, his passion, or both. Could it be that he was not asking the question as a professional journalist but as a man looking for answers for himself?

Not dealing in issues of philosophical truth, Campbell offered his standard explanation, describing such feelings as being of random origin, biological in nature, and without purpose or meaning.

I have to wonder if Moyers was satisfied with Campbell's response. How could he be? The very notion of truth was dismissed as irrelevant, along with his feelings and his question. If I had an opportunity to speak with Mr. Moyers at that moment, my answer would have been "What you are thinking and feeling is truth speaking to you through a story."

If Moyers was dissatisfied with Campbell's response, he would certainly not be alone, for the vast majority of people in this world wonder, like Moyers, "Why do I sense this? And where does this feeling come from?" I

---

[45] Joseph Campbell and Bill Moyers, *The Power of Myth* (New York: MJF Books, Fine Communications, 1988), 44.

believe the answer is that God made us to feel this way and the truth we recognize is his.

Author Brian Godawa spoke to this issue in his book *Hollywood Worldviews*. He wrote,

> Rather than seeing our existence as a series of unconnected random events without purpose, storytelling brings meaning to our lives though the analogy of a carefully crafted plot that reflects the loving sovereignty of the God of the Bible.[46]

Author John Eldredge, in his book *Epic*, echoes Godawa's thoughts when he writes, "People are haunted at some level by a longing to make sense of things."[47] Author Daniel Taylor concurs in his book *The Healing Power of Stories*, when he writes,

> Stories link the past, present and future in a way that tells us where we have been (even before we were born), where we are and where we could be going ... Our stories teach us that there is a place for us and that we fit. They suggest to us that our lives can have a plot. Stories turn mere chronology, one thing after another, into the purposeful action of plot, and thereby into meaning ... Stories are the single best way humans have to account for our experience.[48]

In his famous essay *On Fairy Stories*, Tolkien wrote,

> Tellers of tales who create believable Secondary Worlds enable fantasy to work its wonders. They offer readers a sudden glimpse of the underlying reality of truth. In all such labors writers serve as sub-creators who make,

---

[46] Brian Godawa, *Hollywood Worldviews* (Downers Grove, IL: Intervarsity Press, 2002), 32.
[47] John Eldredge, *Epic* (Nashville, TN: Thomas Nelson, Inc., 2004), 22.
[48] Daniel Taylor, *The Healing Power of Stories* (Dublin: Gill & Macmillan, 1996), 140.

because we are made; and not only made but made in the image and the likeness of a Maker.[49]

Tolkien believed that even in a fictional story, truth could be found if one bothered to look.

Tolkien's good friend C. S. Lewis felt the same way.

Lewis placed a great value on myths, and the making of mythical stories, as one of humanity's primary forms of communicating truth and apprehending reality.[50]

Like the most beloved stories of antiquity, Tolkien's tales of *The Hobbit* and *The Lord of the Rings* have passed the test of time, for they bear the markings of the "One Story" and a universal truth, a truth etched in our minds and hearts by our Creator from the beginning.

This is why we feel so strongly that good should ultimately prevail over evil. This is why we look in our stories for the coming of a hero and why we yearn for the happy ending that this life seldom affords. These enduring stories point to a universal hope that has spanned millennia of human history. A hope that resides in every human heart. The hope revealed in the "One Story."

In his book *The Joyful Christian*, C. S. Lewis observed that all men and women, either consciously or subconsciously, are looking for something more than this life affords, something many never find. He referred to that something as joy and then attempted to define it as an inexplicable desire for something wonderful and perfect but just out of reach. He concluded that his few and fleeting experiences with joy were markers pointing the way toward a mysterious desire for something greater, for which life offered no answers. Like a child looking forward to owning a certain toy, once it is possessed, the intensity of the desire is diminished, and with it, the child's interest in the toy. As we grow older, we continue to search for this

---

[49] J. R. R. Tolkien, *On Fairy Stories* (written in 1938 as an Andrew Lang lecture, [if you keep this word, it's "later," not "latter"] published in 1947), 12, 18, 23.

[50] Terry Glaspey, *The Spiritual Legacy of C.S. Lewis* (Nashville, TN: Cumberland House, 1996), 91.

mysterious commodity, person, or event that will give us joy or happiness, but once we think we've obtained it, we find ourselves disappointed.

Professional athletes often experience an emotional letdown after securing a particular honor or championship. So it is with many things in life. It is as if were looking for something that doesn't exist in this world. Desire is ultimately not satisfied so we keep searching.

We spend our lives seeking something perfect. But it eludes us. We look for perfection in love, but when we find it, love is not as splendid or wonderful as we first thought. We pursue perfection in formal education and the pursuit of a career, but once we have achieved these things, we still are uncertain of our purpose in life. We have children, hoping to fill the void, but as much as we love them, they do not fulfill us. We purchase a house, take vacations, pursue hobbies and leisure, all of which gives us pleasure, yet we still long for more.

As we age, we try to convince ourselves that life has been good to us, that we are satisfied, but in truth, we are not so we continue to look for something we cannot find. We are disappointed, like the child with the toy, for no matter how many toys we possess, our desire is still not satisfied. In the end, our achievements and pleasures are not enough to answer the mysterious longing in our hearts.

C. S. Lewis wrote, "If I find in myself a desire which no experience in this world can satisfy, the most probable explanation is that I was made for another world."[51] I think Lewis was right. I think we are made for another world and the "One Story" is one of many clues pointing to that very reality.

Other intangibles, like love, faith, beauty, and a sense of right and wrong, serve as markers pointing to a metaphysical world we have long since forgotten. A world we consciously or subconsciously long for and search for but struggle to understand or comprehend.

In the book of Romans, Paul the apostle wrote, "People show the requirements of the law are written on their hearts."[52] Solomon wrote, "He [God] has also set eternity in the hearts of men; yet they cannot fathom

---

[51] Walter Martindale and Jerry Rood, eds., *The Quotable Lewis* (Michigan: William B. Eerdmans Publishing Company, 2002), 8.
[52] Romans 2:15.

what God has done from the beginning to the end."[53] Intangibles like moral awareness find their origin in God. Yet we struggle to understand where they came from or what it all means.

God placed these intangibles in the hearts of Tolkien and Lewis as clues to help them recognize and find him. Pieces of eternity were etched in their hearts and minds. That same God put a piece of eternity into each of us as well. These ideas defy definition or scientific explanation. They cannot be proven with mathematical equations or psychological theories or be seen by microscopes or telescopes. But we sense their presence just like Moyer did when he spoke to Campbell about truth.

We recognize these ideas in a story about a struggle between good and evil, the hero's victory, and a happy ending. With this fragment of eternity, God marked us with unique characteristics, setting us apart from all other living creatures, bequeathing to us the clues we need to better understand our divine origin. Humans, according to the book of Genesis, are made in the image of God so for this reason are different from other animals. Man stands alone not only in his moral awareness but also in his capacity to create.

This is why Tolkien referred to humans as "sub-creators" made in the likeness of a Maker. Some, like Tolkien, create stories. Others write symphonies or operas. Still others produce objects of beauty by way of paint or sculpture. Unlike the spider that builds the same web over and over again or the bird that constructs the same nest instinctively, humans demonstrate a unique capacity and inherent inclination to create something new, something beautiful.

Although Webster's dictionary can define the word *beauty*, it cannot tell us what beauty is or where it came from. Why do we recognize it or appreciate it? Why does it touch us and move us to tears? What is its purpose, and why does it matter so much to so many? When a human being looks at a sunset, the ocean, the mountains, or the vast canopy of stars in space, we universally describe these things as "beautiful." No one needs to tell us or teach us this; we seem to know it inherently.

The Bible teaches that beauty, as well as our capacity to recognize and appreciate it, comes from God. With it, he displays his creative power

---

[53] Ecclesiastes 3:11.

and at same time speaks in faint whispers to human hearts that he exists. David the psalmist wrote,

> The heavens declare the glory of God; the skies proclaim the work of his hands. Day after day they pour forth speech; night after night they display knowledge. There is no speech or language where their voice is not heard. Their voice goes out into all the earth, their words to ends of the world.[54]

This is the voice of God speaking to us through the beauty of his creation. People who believe in God recognize him in the inexplicably wonderful things they see in nature.

The concept of beauty serves no discernible purpose in a strictly physical world; however, the fact that beauty exists cannot be denied as it makes up a significant part of human thought and behavior. One must look to the metaphysical world to understand the part beauty plays in human existence.

Like beauty, the "One Story" is intangible yet something we universally recognize and respond to. We are moved by and drawn to it as if it were part of us. We desire it, long for it, and look for it again and again. It gives us hope telling our hearts what we all inherently want to believe: that darkness will ultimately give way to light. Love will be found, hope will be realized, and happiness will be gained in the end.

Whether these stories come in verbal form told around a campfire or written form to become a theatrical play, opera, film, or book, human beings never grow tired of telling or listening to this story of hope. At the root of this fascination is something we call the imagination—another human intangible, like beauty or the "One Story," for which science offers little insight.

Tolkien attributed imagination to God, who made us to be "makers." Armed with this inexplicable commodity, he created the fictitious world of Middle Earth. A place traveled to by tens of millions of readers over the course of half a century. Readers looking for adventure and, more

---

[54] Psalm 19:1–4.

importantly, hope. Through these stories, Tolkien revealed to the world the same great truth pointed to by *Sleepless in Seattle, The Shawshank Redemption, Man of Steel,* and *Home Alone.* Good must always triumph over evil. Darkness will ultimately give way to the light of truth, and love and happiness will be found in the end.

This is the "One Story," God's story for us all. It was the first story, and it shall be the last story. It is the story of the God revealed in the Bible.

For most people, the Bible is too complex to fully understand. Without some historical or cultural context, even people with impressive formal educations can find themselves at a loss when trying to make sense of it. With these things in mind, I would like to offer you a brief synopsis of the Bible in the form of a short story. Having studied the document for nearly fifty years, this, to the best of my understanding, is the story the Bible tells.

Before anything was, before time itself, a single God existed. God was holy and good and His heart was full of love. In the beginning, God created the universe and everything in it: galaxies, stars, and a seemingly endless number of worlds. Because it was in God's heart to create, he fixed his eye on a single world, a tiny blue planet placed in a perfect spot to receive just enough light and warmth from a nearby star to suit his purposes. He made that world green with life and then filled its oceans with living creatures of every sort. In like fashion, he created all the animals that walked on the earth and the birds that flew in the skies. Though all these things pleased him, God was not satisfied. He longed for a being like himself, one he could love and who could love him back. So he created a man and a woman and gave them volition so they could choose to love him because real love is a choice that can only be made freely. God placed them in a garden he called Eden.

In Eden dwelt another being. He was neither an animal nor a man. Lucifer was his name. He was an angel who had once lived with God in the great celestial realm called heaven. Angels were created by God to be his servants and companions, like the man and woman God gave the angels the right to choose. Lucifer was the most beautiful angel in heaven, but his beauty filled his heart with pride so in time he sought to usurp God's throne. In this moment, evil was born. Evil is anything that stands in opposition to God's love and truth. Lucifer gathered a third of the all the angels in heaven and rebelled. God put down the insurrection and banished Lucifer and his followers to the earth, and for this, Lucifer hated God.

Knowing God loved the man and woman, Lucifer sought to deceive them. Appealing to their pride and their right to choose, he tempted them to sin as he and the fallen angels had. The man and woman followed suit, exercising their will against the will of God, choosing to go their own way. In so doing, they rebelled against God's truth and his love. This grieved God deeply, and though he still loved them, he was forced to banish them from the garden because he was a holy God who could not in any way tolerate evil.

Because of what the man and woman did, all the world was changed. What once was perfect now became flawed, and what once was eternal would now become finite, existing in the shadow of decay and death. Time, once of no consequence, would now dictate the end of all living things for all of life would now exist under its dark shadow. The world God had made for the man and woman would be forever marred by their terrible choice. The evil they embraced permeated and poisoned the world. So the earth was cursed because the man and woman rejected the truth and love of God. But God still loved them so he offered a hope of redemption for them, their decedents, and even the earth he had made.

To Lucifer who had done this terrible thing by deceiving the man and woman, God spoke a prophecy that from the descendants of Adam and Eve he would raise up a hero to undo what Satan had done. At the hero's coming, Lucifer would recognize and fear him, striking at him with all his might, but it would be to no avail. God's deliverer would crush Satan and his hosts, putting an end to all the evil he had brought into the world.

The deliverer who would end the curse and destroy evil would also be the hope of redemption promised to the man and woman. Through him they would find forgiveness, healing, hope, and love, and their broken relationship with God would be restored as would His creation. Humankind would again live eternally in the great celestial realm of heaven. This same hope would be extended to any and all who embraced the truth and love of God.

These events set in motion a great conflict between good and evil. Knowing his time was short and fearing the deliverer, Lucifer and his fallen host worked tirelessly to deceive the minds of humankind. At the same time, God and his followers worked to spread the message of his truth that people should love and worship the one true God and love each other as they love themselves, treating each other in the same way they would hope to be treated. Those who believed this truth and sought to live by it looked always in hope for the coming of the deliverer, the restoration of the world, and the end of evil.

Centuries passed and the conflict grew and all suffered, both the children of darkness and the children of light. Wars, disease, pestilence, poverty, and starvation marked the passing of time. God's children persisted in sharing the truth, love, and forgiveness of God, while those who followed Lucifer propagated another idea, a dark and terrible lie. That life was best lived in the pursuit of power, wealth, and pleasure, offering to the children of the world another god to follow, a false god. So the two kingdoms grew together, one against the other, always in opposition, always at war, good against evil.

In the course of time, the first part of God's prophecy against Lucifer came to fruition. The deliverer was born into the world in a miraculous way that marked Him as different from all other men. His mother and father called him Jesus. Lucifer recognized him immediately and sought his destruction as an infant but failed. Three decades would pass. During this time, Lucifer would employ all his power and deceit to undo and destroy the deliverer, but he could not.

For thirty years, Jesus taught, did miracles, and preached his father's truth. Many people were persuaded and God's kingdom grew, and for this, Lucifer hated God all the more. Unknown to Lucifer, Jesus had not come to only spread the truth of God, nor had he come to destroy evil at this time. He had come to give his own life a ransom, to pay the price for humankind's sin. The evil that deceived the hearts and minds of people could only be forgiven by this special gift of God. To achieve this, God would give a piece of himself, his beloved son, Jesus, the Christ. In a sense, a portion of God's goodness would be used to cancel the evil of sin in the hearts of men and women. Only then could fellowship be restored between God and humankind. This was part of God's plan for the redemption of humanity and the first part of fulfilling his prophecy against Lucifer. It would provide forgiveness and grace for all those who confessed their sin and chose to believe in and follow the one true God.

Lucifer did not understand this, for he was not as wise as God. So he plotted how he might kill Jesus, not knowing that in so doing that he would accomplish God's ends and seal his own doom. So Lucifer and his followers deceived the hearts of many, and the Romans and the Jews took Jesus and crucified him on a cross. So Lucifer struck Jesus with all his might as God's prophecy had foretold, but it would be to no avail.

The deliverer was dead and his followers scattered like frightened sheep, and those who loved him most grieved and wept. They took his body and placed it in a tomb, and for a time, all hope seemed lost. Those who were closest to him had heard him speak of his own death and how God would raise him up, but few believed it. On the third day, just as Jesus had prophesied, they came to the tomb and found it empty. By the power of God, Jesus had overcome the power of death and secured a way for the people of the world to once again be right with God.

The first part of the prophecy of God's redemption for humankind was now fulfilled. After a short time of revealing himself to his followers in his risen form, Jesus returned to his Father. But before he departed, he promised he would return and fulfill the rest of the prophecy, restoring all things when God deemed the time to be right.

Lucifer, now understanding his error, feared and hated God all the more and swore revenge on the people of the earth, whom God loved, and particularly on those who severed and loved the risen Christ. So he deceived the Romans, filling their hearts with his own fear and hatred for those called Christians, so named because they served God's deliverer, the Christ.

In the persecution that followed, Christians were imprisoned, tortured, and executed in cruel and barbaric ways, yet because they had seen with their own eyes the risen Christ, they persisted in sharing the truth of God for they no longer feared death. In spite of this persecution, the earthly kingdom of God continued to grow, spreading God's message of truth and love from one end of the Roman Empire to the other. After these events, the conflict between good and evil continued to rage for centuries, even to this very day. So believers looked in hope for the return of the deliverer and the final fulfilment of the prophecy.

(This concludes the first part of the story the Bible tells, spanning both the Old Testament and New Testament. The story is completed in the final book of the Bible, "The Revelation of John." In it, the apostle provides a prophetic glimpse into the final years of human history (i.e., the future and the end of time).)

Knowing that his time is short and that the return of the deliverer was inevitable, Lucifer, for hate's sake, accelerates his efforts. God's followers continue to share his truth that people should love God and each other as they love themselves, but their efforts are dwarfed by the power of and message of darkness. With each passing century, humankind is more deceived by Lucifer's lies as they are consumed by their own desires. The pursuit of power, wealth, and above all pleasure would fill their hearts until there is little room for anything else. The great churches of the earth would stand empty, forgotten relics of the past, dead or dying, because of lack of interest. Humanity would become a god to itself as the memory of a loving God faded from the minds of those who were deceived. As time wanes and end draws near, the world unites, sharing a single economy, a single religion, and a single leader. Referred to only as "the Beast," this leader will be greatly loved and feared; he will possess complete power and no one will be able to stand against him. Unknown to the world, Lucifer will speak through this leader to deceive humankind one last time, closing their ears and eyes to God's love and truth. This he will do to exact his revenge against God and his deliverer.

As a result of Satan's efforts, Christians will again be singled out and persecuted, as they were by the Romans. Because the children of light will not compromise what they believe and because they will not follow the "the Beast" or his teachings, they will suffer as their ancestors did. The darkness of Lucifer's mind and heart will cover the face of the earth with evil until all hope seems lost. At that exact moment, at the end of all things, he will come, the deliverer, the Christ, the hero of old, and with him, the armies of heaven, legends of angels, and saints long forgotten. He will ride on a white horse, wielding a sword followed by a great host, and he will vanquish all of his enemies, fulfilling the prophecy spoken by his Father against Lucifer. Evil will be no more, the curse of decay and death will be ended, the world will be restored to its former glory, and creation itself will rejoice once again to be ruled by a just a loving God.

Those who rejected God's love and persecuted God's people will be cast into darkness, never to be seen again. Those who followed the light and truth of God will be rewarded and come and go freely between the celestial realm of heaven and an earth made new and green again; they will forever dwell with God in perfect peace and joy, and He with them. And Christ will sit on the throne.

This is the story the Bible tells.

I believe that human beings care about this story because God placed something in us that not only recognizes it but desires it above all other stories. The "One Story" reveals the plight of humankind and our collective hope for salvation. In short, it points us back to our Creator.

CHAPTER SIX

ONE AUTHOR

The 2011 Marvel Studios film *Thor,* directed by Kenneth Branagh, paints a familiar picture, telling the story of a god who came to earth to save humankind. Exiled from his celestial home of Asgard by his father Odin, played by Anthony Hopkins, the mighty Thor, portrayed, by Chris Hemsworth, is stripped of his power and forced to live as a mortal on earth. In his absence, his father falls ill and lingers in a deep sleep. Thor's evil brother, Loki, played by Tom Hiddleston, seizes the throne. He proceeds to plot against his now powerless brother as well as the helpless people of earth. To accomplish his evil plan, Loki sends a living suit of armor, a technological terror impervious to man's weapons, to find and kill Thor.

Without his strength or his great hammer, Thor is powerless to stop the "Destroyer" or protect the world's people. In a deliberate act of self-sacrifice, Thor offers his life as a ransom for the people of the earth, imploring Loki to spare their lives and instead take his. The metal giant strikes Thor down with a single blow. Broken and bleeding, he lies dying in the dust. His sweetheart, Jane Foster, played by Natalie Portman, runs to his side and falls weeping on to his chest. Struggling for breath, Thor speaks his last words. "It is over. You are safe."[55] Then he smiles and gasps

---

[55] *Thor,* directed by Kenneth Branagh (Paramount Pictures 2011).

his last breath. Like the Christ who said, "It is finished,"[56] the mighty Thor dies a hero's death. Then something unexpected and wonderful happens.

In Asgard, Thor's father, Odin, still in a deep sleep, is somehow aware of his son's sacrifice. A single tear courses down his old face, and in that moment, his life power is extended to his son. Thor's hammer flies to his hand and the life he willingly forfeited for the world is restored. Instantly and miraculously, he is arrayed in his armor, rising in glory, and is resurrected from the dead. A great battle ensues. Evil is defeated, love and hope are restored, and the theater erupts into applause.

Campbell observed, "The death and resurrection of a savior figure is a common motif in all of these legends."[57]

Balder, another son of Odin, also played a Christlike role.

> Portrayed as a loving and gentle soul, who spread light and good will wherever he went, inevitably, he evoked the envy of his brother Loki, who plotted his tragic death. Balder was similar to the myths of the Egyptian Osiris, the Sumerian Tammuz, and Adonis who was the dying-and-rising god of the ancient Greeks, which they adopted from the Phoenicians. The Germanic peoples believed that the return of wounded, dying Balder would occur in new world, a green land risen from the sea. Balder was expected to return and rule over a world cleansed by catastrophe. It would seem that some of the initial appeal of Christianity in northern Europe was connected with the triumphant return of the risen Christ on Judgment Day.[58]

The similarities to Christianity are uncanny, considering the biblical ideas of the Second Coming of Christ, Judgment Day, and the restoration of the earth's environment depicted in the book of Revelation.

---

[56] John 19:30.

[57] Joseph Campbell and Bill Moyers, *The Power of Myth* (New York: MJF Books, Fine Communications, 1988), 131.

[58] Arthur Cotterell and Rachel Storm, *The Ultimate Encyclopedia of Mythology* (Hermes House, Anness Publishing Ltd., 1999), 184–185.

The same story is told repeatedly in the superhero films of the past decade. Movies like *Captain America, Batman vs. Superman,* and *The Lord of the Rings: The Two Towers* depict the sacrificial death of the hero and his subsequent resurrection. C. S. Lewis commented on these apparent similarities.

> The heart of Christianity is a myth, which is also a fact ... We pass from a Balder or an Osiris, dying nobody knows when or where, to a historical person crucified under Pontius Pilate. By becoming fact, it does not cease to be a myth: that is the miracle.[59]

At the beginning of Peter Jackson's *The Lord of the Rings: The Fellowship of the Ring,* the narrator tells a short history of the one ring of power. He states that the ring had been lost for over two thousand years and become all but forgotten.

> Much that once was, is lost, for none now live who remember it ... And some things that should not have been forgotten were lost. History became legend. Legend became myth.[60]

With the passing of time, people forget certain events and details. What was once known to be true becomes an old wives' tale.

In Tolkien's story, when the ring is found, what was known as myth becomes reality. When Jesus came into this world, lived, died, and was resurrected, the myth of the dying god became a reality.

But long before Jesus came on the scene, the world was looking for answers to the problem of evil. Their fears and hopes found expression in a story passed on verbally for thousands of years before it was recorded in written form. The story is told in what many consider to be the first book ever written, the biblical book of Genesis.

---

[59] Terry Glaspey, *The Spiritual Legacy of C. S. Lewis* (Nashville, TN: Cumberland House, 1996), 91.
[60] *The Lord of the Rings: The Fellowship of the Ring,* directed by Peter Jackson (2001, New Line Productions).

Before Genesis was written, the "One Story" was already deeply ingrained in the human subconscious. To understand its origin, we must go back to the very beginning of religious thought. This starts with the idea of a single God.

In 1859, Charles Darwin's book *On the Origin of Species* brought the theory of evolution to the forefront of scientific thought. It also gave rise to a theological and sociological debate. Did man first believe in a single god, or did the concept of a single god evolve as a result of polytheism (a belief in many gods)?

> Other thinkers, working more or less concurrently with Darwin, hoped that the principles of evolution would enable them to unlock mysteries of another kind of phenomena—the origins of human society, culture and religion. How did this particular group of scholars propose to explain the origin of something so complex as religion, for example, on an evolutionary model? First they dismissed the Bible's claim that the first religion to appear on Earth was a monotheistic faith—a faith which the one true God has confirmed since antiquity with successive revelations. Nor did they accept another biblical insistence, that spiritism and polytheism in all their forms are "false" religions resulting from man's perverse attempts to remold the original "true" religion after his own misguided preference. In other words evolutionist erased distinctions between "true" and "false" religion as scientifically meaningless. Lumping all religions in the same crucible, they advanced the bold hypothesis: that the very religions the Bible calls "false" originated first![61]

The most prominent among these atheistic thinkers was an Englishman by the name of Edward B. Tylor, who offered a compelling theory in his work *Primitive Culture: Researches into the Development of Mythology, Philosophy, Religion, Art and Custom.* Tylor speculated that "the idea of

---

[61] Don Richardson, *Eternity in Their Hearts* (Bloomington, MN: Bethany House Publishers, 1981), 118.

the human 'soul' must have been the natural seed thought from which all other religious concepts evolved."[62]

His argument went something like this: Ancient peoples imagined that they had souls because of the shared biological experiences of things like sleep, illness, ecstasy, and death. These mysteries, coupled with dreams and visions, caused them to speculate about a soul. In the course of time, they noticed their shadows and their own reflections in the water; these things reinforced their suspicions. Over time, these people speculated about the possibility that other entities found in nature—like trees, mountains, or rivers—might also possess souls. This was the first religion.

As centuries passed, culture developed a stratification of classes: peasants and aristocrats. The idea of some people being superior to or ruling over others gave rise to the notion of polytheism: many gods, some great and some small. In time, one aristocrat rose above all others to become a monarch, king, or pharaoh. This ultimately gave rise to the idea of one great god (monotheism).

> At least four notions were implicit in Tylor's evolutionary model. First, there was no longer anything mysterious about religion; religion's natural origin and subsequent evolutionary development now having been scientifically explained. Second, since monotheism marked the final stage in religion's evolution, religion had now reached the end of a dead-end street. Third, further developments in human society were already dictating the next step for people who wanted to stay on the crest of evolution's wave: abandon religion with it's now defunct God, gods or spirits. What then was the fourth notion implicit in Tylor's theory? It was the one which would make it possible to test the validity of Tylor's thesis by field research. If Tylor was correct, primitive societies would be devoid of monotheistic presuppositions, since class stratification and

---

[62] Edward B. Tylor, *Primitive Culture: Researches into the Development of Mythology, Philosophy, Religion, Art and Custom* (London: John Murray Publishers Ltd., 1871).

the later concept of monarchy had not yet developed to prompt the notion of monotheism.[63]

In field study, Tylor's argument fell apart. Research of the most primitive cultures on earth repeatedly revealed the truth that all religious thought began with a single god, often referred to as the "skygod." Researchers like Father Wilhelm Schmidt, E. De Pressense, and a student of Tylor's named Andrew Lang discovered that time and time again, a single creative god was at the root of the most primitive religious thought.

> Schmidt began documenting and compiling evidence for "native monotheism," evidence which was now beginning to flow like a tide from all parts of the world. In 1912 [the year of Lang's death], Schmidt published his mammoth *Ursprung Der Gottesidee (The Original Concept of God)*. Still more data kept pouring in, so he published another volume, and another, and another, until by 1955, he had accumulated more than 4,000 pages of evidence in a total of 12 large volumes! The entire thirteenth chapter of Schmidt's *The Origin and Growth of Religion* is devoted to quotations from dozens of anthropologists, showing that acceptance of Schmidt's research was virtually universal.[64]

Amazingly, forms of Tylor's argument continued to be taught in the atheistic regimes of both the Soviet Union and Red China for decades after it was discredited.

Having established that religious thought began with one god, we will now consider the story of the Christian God.

In the opening pages of the Bible, the "One Story" begins in a garden called Eden. Though a limited number of fossils of modern *Homo sapiens* have been found in various places in Africa, most anthropologists agree that human beings had their beginnings somewhere between modern Egypt in northern Africa and the Mesopotamian Valley of the Middle

---

[63] Don Richardson, *Eternity in Their Hearts* (Bloomington, MN: Bethany House Publishers, 1981), 119.
[64] Richardson, 124.

East, near the Tigris and Euphrates rivers. *National Geographic Concise History of the World* says, "Although the story of human evolution and peopling of the planet still holds many mysteries, the most widely accepted theory states that modern humans came out of Africa."[65]

New York Times best-selling author Dr. Yuval Harari provides a similar explanation in his book *Sapiens: A Brief History of Humankind*. He writes, "Scientists agree that about 70,000 years ago, Sapiens from East Africa spread into the Arabian Peninsula, from there they quickly overran the Eurasian landmass."[66]

In addition to the evidence provided by archaeologists, paleontologists, and historians pointing to the same geographical location of man's origin, we can now add the contributions of geneticists. According to *National Geographic Concise History of the World,* geneticist Spencer Wells took blood samples from thousands of men living in isolated tribes around the world and followed the path of the Y-chromosome, which is passed from father to son. Wells discovered that all humans alive today can be traced back to a tribe in Africa.[67] This supports the claim of Genesis that man's history begins in a place the Bible calls Eden. It is here the "One Story" begins.

Because of their rebellion against God, Adam and Eve were forced to leave the Garden of Eden and relocate somewhere to the east, to live as mortals in a world ruled by sin, decay, and death. The sons of Adam moved west, toward modern Israel and Egypt. From that point, humankind migrated to rest of the world. They took with them their tools, their livestock, and the story of what happened in Eden.

The sons of Adam told the story of how Eden was undone by the serpent and how evil entered the world of humans. They also told of the "seed of the woman" who would come someday in the future to crush the serpent's head and end the curse of sin. Since then, people have looked for a hero who would wield the power of a god, revealed in the form of a man, a hero who would end the curse of sin and death.

---

[65] Neil Kagan, *National Geographic Concise History of the World* (The National Geographic Society, 2013), 28.

[66] Yuval Noah Harari, *Sapiens: A Brief History of Humankind* (Harper, an Imprint of HarperCollins Publishers, 2015), 144.

[67] Neil Kagan, *National Geographic Concise History of the World* (The National Geographic Society, 2013), 29.

As time passed, this one story took on many forms but continued to maintain its core components. For millennia, the story was told and retold in oral form, contributing to the many different versions history reveals today.

There is an old parlor game whereby people sitting in a circle take turns whispering a short phrase into the ear of the person sitting next to them. At the end of the game, the last person announces the phrase out loud. The person who started the game reveals the original phrase. Laughter ensues as the two phrases are usually not even remotely related to each other. Such was the case with the "One Story." As it was shared around campfires, in huts and caves, and in crude houses made of mud and stone, it gave rise to numerous variations.

In a commentary on the book of Genesis, Bible scholar Derek Kidner noted,

> Certain epics from Babylonia tell of Creation, others of a Deluge; the most impressive being *The Epic of Atrahasis,* which provides some sort of parallel to Genesis 1–8. However, the book of Genesis starts its account at an earlier point than Atrahasis, and when his accounts come to an end, the Genesis account is barely begun.[68]

Though many cultures have accounts of creation and a great flood, the Genesis story is older than them all, and more complete, thus marking it as the original.

Bible scholar Merrill Unger, in his book *Archaeology and the Old Testament,* wrote,

> These similarities, however remote, may be explained in that they have a common source. The creation story, the fall of man, the great flood, were all historical events that gave rise to variant traditions. Early races of men whenever they wandered, took with them these earliest traditions of mankind, and in varying latitudes and climes have

---

[68] Derek Kidner, *Genesis: An Introduction and Commentary* (InterVarsity Press, 1967), 13.

modified them according to their religions and mode of thought. Modifications as time proceeded, resulted in the corruption of the original pure tradition (or truth). The Biblical narrative, we may conclude, represents the original form these traditions must have assumed.[69]

The story of Genesis, the Bible, and its Christ bears all the marks of the original, the first story, the "One Story," the story Hollywood tells and retells.

In a quick overview of the world's major religions, the author of the "One Story" becomes evident. Buddha neither spoke nor wrote of God, nor did he claim deity for himself; the evil he saw was the material world, and his remedy was detachment from that world. Judaism continues to look for a Messiah, having rejected Jesus as either a liar or a lunatic. In Hinduism each person finds his or her origin in Brahman, who represents "the whole," and life is a process of returning to that whole by means of reincarnation. Confucius promoted a religion of ancestor worship, removing God from the discussion. Islam came on the scene hundreds of years after Christ's death; the Islamic believer saves himself or herself through a system of good deeds and strict obedience. Mohammad's teachings, compiled in the Koran, are a personal reflection on Christian and Hebrew thought reworked to his own way of thinking.

Though each of the world's major religions possesses bits and pieces of truth, none bear all the marks of the original and, therefore, none are complete—with the exception of Christianity. In a sense, the major world religions validate the Christian faith by the fragments of the "One Story" they reveal. No world religion tells the "One Story" more perfectly, more completely than Christianity, and no founder of those religions portrays more precisely Campbell's mythical hero than Jesus, the Christ.

Of course, organized Christianity is not without its flaws. History is replete with the failures of Christ's so-called followers. Events like the Crusades and the Inquisition, not to mention the more recent failures of Catholic and Protestant churches and leaders, certainly give reason to doubt the validity of the Christian message. However, a belief is not made

---

[69] Merrill Unger, *Archeology and the Old Testament* (Zondervan Publishing House, 1954), 37.

untrue or unjust because of the failure of those who claim to represent it. To rightly judge Christianity and the story it tells, one must look at Christ alone, the embodiment of truth.

As for those who have failed to represent him rightly in this world, Jesus said,

> Not everyone who says to me, "Lord, Lord," will enter the kingdom of heaven. Many will say to me on that day, "Lord, Lord, did we not prophesy in your name and in your name drive out demons and in your name perform many miracles?" Then I will tell them plainly, "I never knew you. Away from me, you evildoers!"[70]

Pretenders and hypocrites may claim to represent God and his truth, but that does not make them Christians. Jesus made it clear that they will be punished for their crimes in the end. The flaws and failures of Christianity find their origin in individuals such as these and not in the founder they falsely claim to serve.

Intellectual atheists also recognize that Christianity bears the marks of the original, for they have consistently targeted Christianity in their criticisms and arguments while for the most part ignoring other major world religions. I have always believed that atheists have expended the majority of their efforts to discredit this single faith because they recognize its uniqueness and see it as the greatest threat to their worldview. Christ's life, his deeds, his claim to deity, and the promise of his return make him different from all other so-called messiahs or prophets.

For these reasons and many more, I believe that the author of the "One Story" is the Christian God. If the "One Story" is true, and if its author is the God of Bible, and the hero is Jesus the Christ, those who place their trust in him can look forward to a happy ending to their individual stories—an ending far more glorious and satisfying than Hollywood's finest efforts could ever concoct.

So we will now turn our full attention to this ending, for every good story must have a happy ending.

---

[70] Matthew 7:21–23.

PART THREE

THE CONCLUSION

CHAPTER SEVEN

HAPPILY EVER AFTER

Most people desire a happy ending. But for many, life's harsh realities seem to discount any such hope as childish or unrealistic.

Like the battle between good and evil, the happy ending was not included in Campbell's definition of the hero's journey, even though it was clearly evident. As an intellectual atheist, Campbell's preconceived notions rendered such ideas moot. For Campbell, good and evil were only an opinion and the happy ending nothing short of nonsense. He wrote,

> The fairy tale of happiness ever after cannot be taken seriously; it belongs to the never-never land of childhood, which is protected from the realities that will become terribly known soon enough; just as the myth of heaven ever after is for the old whose lives are behind them and whose hearts have to be readied for the last portal of the transit into night.[71]

For the atheist, there is no God so there can be no heaven, which makes a happy ending out of the question. Many of today's Hollywood elitists would concur with Campbell's assessment, viewing films like *Star*

---

[71] Joseph Campbell, *The Hero with a Thousand Faces* (Princeton, NJ: Princeton University Press, 1949), 28.

Wars and *Sleepless in Seattle* as dumbed-down stories with two-dimensional characters, simplistic plots of good versus evil, and predictable endings that are always happy. With few exceptions, the Academy Awards overlook such films in favor of movies that make some kind of political or social statement or films that are considered in some sense more artistic. But these are not the films that the majority of moviegoers want to see. These are not the stories the human heart longs for.

Several years ago, my wife suggested that we watch the film *Message in a Bottle.* Her interest was that it was a love story and that it stared a young, handsome Kevin Costner. Like any good husband, I secured the film at our local video store and proceeded to plan the evening. As I remember, the film was both well done and reasonably enjoyable. For the most part, the evening went as planned until the end, when the hero died. Most of the time, my wife is a rational and reasonable person who is not given to excessive emotional displays, including fits of rage or anger. She is for the most part an individual of grace and dignity who can master her feelings and passions in any given situation, regardless of how extreme or dire. Not on this night! If I remember correctly, she said, "He's dead? He died? That's it?" What followed quickly dispelled any romantic hopes I might have had for that evening as my thoughts were redirected to damage control for my disappointed and annoyed spouse. My unsuspecting wife had been cheated out of the happy ending she expected and felt she deserved. Having invested $4 on the rental and two hours of her time, sadly it was not to be. And even though I am a burly man who cares little for warm, fuzzy movies, I have to admit I felt cheated too! Now some would say that the ending was realistic, and maybe it was, but it doesn't change how we both felt that night.

Message in a Bottle did poorly at the box office, especially given Costner's considerable popularity at the time. Consequently it is not one of the films for which he will be remembered.

There was another film for which Costner will always be remembered. That film was *Field of Dreams,* which did have a happy ending. It wasn't realistic, and to some people, it didn't even make sense, but to the vast majority of theatergoers, male and female, it was a magical film that touched both their hearts and minds. It was a film that would be remembered. It pointed to a metaphysical world located just at the edge of a cornfield.

The film told those who viewed it that there is more to life and more to us than meets the eye.

Testimony to this fact is the phrase "build it and they will come" used again and again by both journalists and authors, not to mention men and women in daily conversation. This simple phrase has become a part of American culture because the ending of the film was happy and therefore satisfying.

In director David Frankel's film *The Devil Wears Prada*, Academy Award-winning actress Meryl Streep plays the part of Miranda Priestly, the editor of a prominent fashion magazine in New York City. Opposite Streep is Anne Hathaway playing the part of a young woman, Andy Sachs, who lands the job of Miranda's personal assistant. In short order, the film draws a clear line between Miranda (evil) and Andy (good), one being powerful, worldly, and experienced while the other was none of the above. Miranda is portrayed as demanding, arrogant, self-serving, and at times even cruel. Andy is seen as young and naïve and, compared to Miranda, innocent or even pure.

In the first thirty minutes, you quickly learn to hate Miranda, and at the same time, you find yourself both pitying and rooting for Andy. By the end of the film, you realize that it is not Miranda that is evil but the career she has embraced. She is victimized by her own ambition and at the same time made subject to a heartless and impersonal business whose demands were both unreasonable and endless. In due course, Andy is seduced (by the dark side), becoming more and more like Miranda as she begins to embrace the fashion world, forsaking her friends and her old life for the glitz, glamour, and power of Miranda's world. In the end, Andy discovers the emptiness and loneliness of Miranda's life before it's too late, walking away from the job; she chooses instead to return to the life she had forsaken. Good triumphs over evil that Andy is saved from Miranda's fate.

In the animated film *Shrek*, the classic fairy tale is violated almost beyond recognition all for the sake of a laugh, which I have to admit I enjoyed. On one hand, you have an extremely offensive and abrasive ogre (voice by Mike Myers) and his unwanted but faithful sidekick, a talking donkey (Eddie Murphy). Not exactly your typical heroes, but by comparison to Lord Farquaad (voice by John Lithgow), the ogre and donkey come across like saints. Lord Farquaad could best be described as a short and comical version of Darth Vader or Miranda Priestly; take your pick. Lord Farquaad has a kingdom, an army, and an evil plan to marry the beautiful Fiona (Cameron Diaz). Without rehashing the entire film, the heroes triumph over evil with the help of a fire-breathing dragon who swoops in at the last minute and swallows Lord Farquaad in a single bite, which elicited both laughter and cheers from the audience at the conclusion of the film. The ending was happy, and so was everyone in the theater.

In the romantic comedy *My Big Fat Greek Wedding,* Tula (Nia Vardalos) is a lonely, awkward Greek girl with serious self-esteem issues. Though she is loved by her family and works dutifully at the family diner, she longs for more. Tula dreams the same dreams of many young woman: hoping for college, a career, and of course, love. But that just doesn't seem to be in the cards. One day there is a chance meeting with the handsome and single Ian Miller played by John Corbett. What follows is an endearing and delightful comedy of errors depicting family loyalty, cultural differences, and even religion as Ian attempts to pursue Tula despite her father's best efforts to run interference. The evil is that Tula is lonely; she is unsure of her own worth as a woman, and like all human beings, she longs for relationship and love. Good triumphs over evil when Tula finds love with Ian. The pattern is the same.

If the "One Story" is God's story for us all, its happy ending is more than just a fanciful wish and more than just a predictable ending to a film. It's the way things are supposed to be. The happy ending is the truth. It is what God intended for all those who would follow him. We inherently react to it in stories and films because something inside us recognizes it and wants to believe it.

In 1939, two men who worked on Broadway collaborated on a new musical film. E. Y. Harburg was the lyricist, and Harold Arlen composed the music. Of a dozen songs, one seized the hearts and imaginations of audiences across America. Sung by a little girl in pigtails, the words of the song are still remembered today, some eighty years later. The girl was Judy Garland, and the song was "Over the Rainbow." In the opening scene, Dorothy is worried and upset about many things. Her busy aunt tells her, "Help us out today and find yourself a place where you won't get into any trouble!"[72] Dorothy ponders her aunt's request by musing to herself, and to her little dog, Toto, whether there is such a place where there isn't any trouble. She concludes that there must be. "It's not a place you can get to by a boat or a train. It's far, far away ... behind the moon ... beyond the rain."[73] Dorothy then breaks into song about a wonderful place where troubles melt away and dreams come true.

Though Judy Garland will always be remembered for singing the iconic song, the words will forever belong to Harburg. Though the lyrics were meant to portray the feelings of a little girl, they came from the mind of a grown man. The question is this: where do such thoughts come from? Like millions of artists, poets, theologians, musicians, and philosophers before him, Harburg expressed in his lyrics the inherently human idea or belief that something better than the life we know must exist. Native Americas dubbed it the Happy Hunting Grounds, Christians refer to it as heaven, and the ancient Greeks and Romans called it Elysium. Such is the case with thousands of cultures throughout human history, each one looking for the answer, looking for a place "somewhere over the rainbow" where the pain of life is left behind in favor of a new paradigm defined by joy and peace.

The Oscar for best picture in the year 2000 went to *Gladiator,* a grim and graphic story of betrayal and loss depicting one man's journey to Elysium. His wife and son are brutally murdered and he is betrayed and sold as slave to a man who trained gladiators for profit. Russell Crowe plays Roman general Maximus Decimus Meridius, and Djimon Hounsou plays fellow slave Juba. Early one morning, Maximus is seated on a stonewall as Juba approaches from behind, staring at the distant horizon and waving his huge black hand across the panorama of the sky. Juba says, "It is somewhere out there, my country, my home. My wife is preparing food and my daughter carries water from the river. Will I ever see them again? I think no." Maximus responds, "Do you believe you will see them again when you die?" "I think so," says Juba, "but then, I will die soon. They will not die for many years. I will have to wait." To which Maximus says, "But you would wait?" "Of course," Juba responds. Then hesitating for

---

[72] *The Wizard of Oz,* directed by Victor Fleming and George Cukor (Warner Bros. Pictures, 1939).

[73] *The Wizard of Oz.*

just a moment, Maximus reveals the pain of his personal loss when he says to Juba, "You see, my wife and son are already waiting for me." Smiling reassuringly, Juba responds, "You will meet them again."[74]

The scene tears at the heart for it lays bare a hope that most people inherently cling to, one that reaches beyond both death and reason: the hope of a home we have never known but desperately need to believe exists. The film concludes with one final contest in the great Colosseum in Rome. Maximus, though victorious, is fatally wounded and lies in the dust while gasping out his last words. Evil is defeated, justice is secured, but his life is now forfeit as is the case with so many heroes. Lucilla, a daughter of Caesar played by Connie Nielsen, runs to him, kneeing in the dirt, in an expression of compassion and pity, knowing both his loss and his pain. She simply says, "Go to them."

The scene now shifts and Maximus stands before a great gate. The camera focuses on his soiled and bloodied hand as it pushes the door of gate open. Now, for the first time, his weary face smiles ever so slightly as he beholds the Elysian Fields. Walking through the tall grass, he sees his home and his wife in the distance as his son runs toward him on a dirt road; then the picture fades away. He is home. The ending is happy, as it should be, the pain and suffering of his life is finished, and all that now lies before him are peace and joy.

When we read a book or view a film that portrays some form of this story, something deep inside us responds with hope and joy. These happy endings provide more than just a passing feeling of satisfaction. Tolkien explained these fictional moments as "a sudden glimpse of the underlying reality of truth."[75] They point to something real, something tangible, something that could be gained.

The rush you get when the hero is victorious over evil, when justice is secured, when love is found and everybody lives happily ever after, is more than just a feeling. It is a transmission from God to that piece of eternity he placed in you. Like an electrical current, it makes a connection, sending a message to your subconscious that life is more than it seems and that there is more to you than meets the eye: that God exists and that heaven is real.

---

[74] *Gladiator,* directed by Ridley Scott (DreamWorks and Universal Studios, 2003).
[75] Verlyn Flieger, *Tolkien on Fairy-Stories* (HarperCollins UK, 2014).

In that moment, the door to the metaphysical world is cracked open ever so slightly and we are permitted to peek inside.

Even when we know the story is fiction, its undeniable power fills our hearts and we sense its truth. We recognize something that we desperately want to believe is real, something we know in our hearts is right: that good must triumph over evil. The happy ending to a film stirs this desire—sometimes faintly, other times with considerable force. C. S. Lewis spoke of this experience as being "only a kind of copy, or echo, or mirage."[76] He said, "Earthly pleasures [like films or stories] were never meant to satisfy it, but only to arouse it, to suggest the real thing."[77] The "real thing" is the heaven of the Bible, the happy ending to the "One Story," which Lewis said "he would not find until after death."[78]

Paul the apostle wrote of this experience in the New Testament. "For now we see only a reflection as in a mirror: then we shall see face to face. Now I know in part; then I shall know fully, even as I am fully known."[79] The mirrors of Paul's day did not provide the clear image we see in mirrors today. The ancient mirror was a highly polished piece of metal whose image was fuzzy and distorted. Paul was saying, "I see God, but not clearly. Someday I will see him as he is, just as he sees me." This was Paul's hope: the hope of life after death.

The happy ending we experience in films is that mirror. We gaze into it again and again, looking for something we cannot find in this world, seeing fuzzy images of a reality we do not fully understand. Looking for someone to save us, to forgive and love us, and to make what is wrong in this world right. Tolkien observed, "The particular quality of the 'joy' in successful Fantasy can thus be explained as a sudden glimpse of the underlying reality of truth. It is not only a 'consolation' for the sorrow of this world, but a satisfaction and an answer to that question, 'Is it true?'"[80]

The "One Story," with its happy ending, is indeed true for all those who put their faith in the Christian God.

The joy of which Tolkien spoke is that experience of euphoria at the

---

[76] C. S. Lewis, *Mere Christianity* (Macmillan Publishing Company, 1943), 120.

[77] Lewis, 120.

[78] Lewis, 120.

[79] 1 Corinthians 13:12.

[80] Verlyn Flieger, *Tolkienon Fairy-Stories* (HarperCollins UK, 2014).

end of the movie when good triumphs over evil. We instinctively rejoice at the triumph of light over darkness. The pleasurable experience of a happy ending is a marker pointing to heaven, and the happy ending God provides for the penitent heart.

A key component of the happy ending is the overcoming of an ever-growing darkness. Only when evil seems insurmountable does the hero achieve his decisive victory. In the Westerns of my childhood, the cavalry always arrived, when all seemed lost, just in the nick of time. In Peter Jackson's *The Lord of the Rings,* evil threatened to envelop all of Middle Earth. In George Lucas's *Star Wars,* evil grows to gargantuan proportions, threatening galaxies, and in Hollywood's latest offering, *Avengers: Infinity War,* a new villain sets his sights on the entire universe. In all of these stories, resolution is not found until the very end.

The biblical storyline is the same. The darkness of evil pushes back the light of truth until all would seem hopeless. This is exactly what the Bible teaches will happen. It refers to this time as "the last days," the end of the story. Paul the apostle wrote,

> There will be terrible times in the last days. People will be lovers of themselves, lovers of money, boastful, proud, abusive, disobedient to their parents, ungrateful, unholy, without love, unforgiving, slanderous, without self-control, brutal, not lovers of the good, treacherous, rash, conceited, lovers of pleasure, rather than lovers of God.[81]

The apostle Peter wrote,

> In the last days scoffers will come, scoffing and following their own evil desires. They will say, "Where is this 'coming' he [Christ] promised? Ever since our fathers died, everything goes on as is has since the beginning of creation."[82]

Paul summed up humankind's future when he wrote,

[81] 2 Timothy 3:1–4.
[82] 2 Peter 3:3–4.

There is going to come a time when people won't listen to the truth, but will go around looking for teachers who will tell them just what they want to hear. They won't listen to what the Bible says but will blithely follow their own misguided ideas.[83]

Christianity is losing the battle for the hearts and minds of humankind. We are losing more decisively with each passing decade, and that is simply the truth.

But according to the scriptures, at the end of this growing pattern of rejection, the hero will come, turning what would appear to be a sure disaster into triumph. Christ will return, in the nick of time, to save the world from darkness.

Tolkien, who loved the study of historical linguistics, coined a new word to describe this exact scenario: "eucatastrophe."[84] By adding the prefix *eu*, which means "good," to the word *catastrophe,* Tolkien defined that wonderful moment when something unexpected happens and defeat is miraculously turned to triumph.

Super Bowl XLIX provided a "eucatastrophe" moment. Twenty-six seconds before the end of the game, a Seattle wide receiver caught a miraculous pass, all but guaranteeing a Seahawks victory while at the same time sealing the apparent doom of New England. But a few moments later, an interception in the end zone cemented a Patriots win. A catastrophe for Seattle fans and a eucatastrophe for the fans of the New England Patriots, never to be forgotten.

In Tolkien's *The Lord of the Rings,* the forces of Middle Earth strive valiantly against the power of the enemy, but with each successive effort, their situation grows worse. In acts of sacrifice and bravery, they struggle against the darkness, but with each battle, their numbers are further depleted. In the end, it is clear that they cannot win. For all of their love, courage, strength, and resolve, they are unable to stand before the endless hosts of Mordor and the seemingly limitless power of Sauron.

Two tiny hobbits, Frodo and Sam, make their way deep into the

---

[83] 2 Timothy 4:3–4.
[84] Verlyn Flieger, *Tolkien on Fairy-Stories* (HarperCollins UK, 2014), 22.

enemy's land, bearing the ring of power that had once belonged to the dark lord. Their mission is to cast the ring into the fires of Mount Doom, where it would once and for all be destroyed, putting an end to Sauron's power.

The remaining heroes of the story lead the armies of Middle Earth to stand before the black gates, challenging the dark lord to one final battle. They know they cannot win. Their goal is to be a diversion, to distract Sauron's watchful eye in their direction, buying precious time with their lives so that Frodo and Sam can reach the mountain undetected and complete their task.

What remains of the armies of men assemble before the black gates, their flags flying proudly. They issue their challenge to the dark lord. The gates open slowly, and from them issue forth all the hosts of Mordor. In a matter of minutes, the tiny army is surrounded by a force ten times its size.

At this moment, the scene shifts back to Mount Doom, where to Sam's horror Frodo is overcome by the evil of the ring, deciding not to destroy it at the last moment but to keep it for himself. All seems lost.

At that same moment, the creature Gollum, who also desired the power of the ring, attacks Frodo in a final effort to regain his lost treasure. They fight on the edge of a great cliff just above the molten fires of Mount Doom. As they struggle, Gollum bites off the finger that bears the ring. Frodo falls to the ground in pain, grasping his wounded hand. Gollum dances in delight. As he gloats over his prize, he steps too close to the edge before falling over the brink with a shriek. Gollum and the ring plunge into molten fire, the power of Sauron is broken, and the battle before the gates of Mordor turns from defeat to victory as the hosts of Mordor flee in confusion and fear. The men of the west rejoice in knowing that the ring bearer has fulfilled his quest.

John Davenport, professor of philosophy at Fordham University, comments,

> Then comes perhaps the most poignant moment in the whole text. Sam sees Frodo, pale and worn, and yet himself again; and in his eyes there was peace now, neither strain or will, nor madness, nor any fear. His burden was taken away. There was his dear master of the sweet days in the Shire. "Master!" cried Sam, and fell upon his knees. In all

the ruin of the world for the moment he felt only joy, great joy. The burden was gone. His master had been saved: he was himself again, he was free.[85]

On the verge of utter ruin, at the end of hope, something unexpected reverses the fortunes of all. Good prevails over evil, and a dark and terrible ending is transformed into victory, peace, and joy unimaginable. This is Tolkien's eucatastrophe. This is the triumph of the hero.

This echoes the joy of those believers who witnessed Christ's resurrection as death was turned to life. This same joy will be experienced by all who witness Christ's return at the end of time and evil's final destruction.

In his essay "On Fairy-Stories," Tolkien argued that the historical events of the gospel narratives are shaped by God, the master story maker, "having a structure of the sudden turn from catastrophe to most satisfying and of all happy endings, a structure shared by the best of human stories."[86] The true happy ending is more than just happy; it is joyful, which is deeper and more profound. Happiness is fleeting as it comes and goes with circumstance and time. But joy can be present even in the face of great tragedy and loss, and joy is often expressed in tears as it touches something inside us.

In Disney's *Mary Poppins,* Mr. Banks (David Tomlinson) is facing what he believes to be the end of his world when he is summoned by the officers of the bank to attend a late-night meeting. The purpose is no mystery to Banks, who fully expects to be dismissed from his job. He walks to the bank alone, through the dark streets of London, while contemplating the worst. Upon arrival he is ushered into the boardroom to meet with the president and the partners. The scene that follows is intended to mimic a dishonorable discharge from the military. Seasoned with creative elements of humor, Banks is disgraced before his peers and then ceremoniously dismissed. It is at this moment, when all sees lost, that Banks comes to a personal revelation: that his family is more important

---

[85] John Davenport, *The Lord of the Rings and Philosophy* (Open Court Publishing Company, a division of Carus Publishing Company, 2003), 216.
[86] Colin Duriez, *Tolkien and C. S. Lewis: The Gift of Friendship* (Hidden Spring, an imprint of Paulist Press, 2003), 54.

than his position at the bank. He realizes that Mary Poppins was right all along and that life was more than just work and personal achievement. In that instant, his sad countenance is replaced with a broad grin stretching from ear to ear. He attempts to share his discovery with the officers of the bank while laughing uncontrollably. The officers think him "mad." Undaunted, he turns away and dances out of the boardroom and into the street, a new and better man.

Returning home, he descends to his basement to look for the kite that the children had broken earlier in the story and he had previously had neither the time nor the interest to fix. Emerging from the cellar, he greets his wife with the news he has been fired and then reveals to the children the kite he has lovingly repaired. When asked by his children how he did it, Banks responds by singing the song "Let's Go Fly a Kite." One by one, the family joins in, singing with him, and then off they go to the park, out the door, and down the street together while singing the iconic song. When they reach the park, the Banks family finds all the officers of the bank, who are now flying kites of their own, having apparently adopted Mr. Bank's change of heart. They proceeded to commend Banks for his astute insight and reinstate him with a promotion, and all is right with the world.

Written words cannot do justice as to the impact of this closing scene. For years its power baffled me as I struggled to hold back tears watching the Banks family dance down the street hand in hand. It seemed silly that I, as a grown man, should be so moved by such a simple film and such a transparent ending. In reality, however, what I was watching was more than just the happy ending to a clever story. I was witnessing the restoration of a family and experiencing the joy of watching their lives set free from a subtle, almost invisible evil that once held them captive.

The Bible teaches that this same happy ending can be experienced by anyone who is willing to embrace God's truth and follow Christ. However dark, flawed, or lonely your earthly existence is, there is a reason to hope for something better in Christ—a happy ending to your own story.

The biblical narrative reveals a happy ending first on the personal level and then on a global scale. Before we can wrap our heads around a God who will save the world, we must first experience his salvation as individuals.

In the second volume of Tolkien's *The Lord of the Rings* trilogy, we are introduced to Theoden, king of Rohan and leader of the horse riders. His personal history is left to the imagination except for one thing: the self-doubt that ever gnawed at his mind. Though we are given no reason to believe that Theoden was not a good leader, he saw himself as a lesser king than his sires. He had never led his nation into any great battles or won any wars. During his reign, the nation of Rohan had grown weak, living in the shadow of more powerful enemies.

Theoden fell under the spell of an evil wizard. In his debilitated condition, the king relinquished his power to rule, which allowed his closest counselor the opportunity to betray him and wreak havoc in the kingdom.

When his only son is killed in a skirmish with enemies of Rohan, Theoden blames himself. In time, the king is freed from the evil spell, but even in his right mind, he continues to struggle with what he sees as his own failures and inadequacies.

Until the day fate calls him to one final battle on the Plennor Fields before the gates of the capital city of Gondor. Hopelessly outnumbered, he leads his army of horse riders into a battle they have little chance of winning. The old king seeks not only glory but, more importantly, personal redemption. This is a chance for Theoden to prove himself, to make things right, and to finally lay to rest the demons of his past.

Beyond all hope, his men prevail, but the king is mortally wounded. As he lay dying, he says to one of the hobbits, "My body is broken. I go to my fathers. And even in their mighty company I shall not now be ashamed."[87] Theoden dies with peace and hope, no longer ashamed of himself or his life, feeling for the first time that he was a king worthy of remembrance. His failures are erased and his life redeemed. What was wrong is made right. So he smiles, even as he draws his last breath, satisfied in the end.

Is this not the happy ending we all hope for? Not to die in battle but for our lives to find validation, a sense of worth, to know that all our failures are forgiven and that we can even forgive ourselves. That we can die at peace with ourselves and with God.

---

[87] J. R. R. Tolkien, *The Return of the King* (New York: Houghton Mifflin Company, 2002), 852.

Like the old king, most of us are haunted by self-doubt or fear that is rooted in our personal shortcomings or failures. In the same way we recognize the evil in the world around us, we also sense evil in our own lives—and we are powerless to overcome it. We wish we could be more self-controlled, more loving, less judgmental, or just "better." But for all our efforts, we remain very much the same.

This inherent need to be restored or redeemed explains our interest in stories that follow the pattern of the "One Story." We search for a hero to save us. To love us. To free us from loneliness, doubt, and fear and to forgive our failures and lift us up. To change us and make us new. To take us in his arms and tell us that everything is going to be all right. This is what Christ offers.

Award-winning screenwriter Brian Godawa observed that movies

> narrate the events surrounding characters who overcome obstacles to achieve some goal and who in the process, are confronted with their personal need for change. In short, movie storytelling is about redemption—the recovery of something lost or the attainment of something needed.[88]

For most of us, the redemption we seek has to do with personal flaws we can't seem to shake. Fictional heroes often reflect these same imperfections.

Many times, as movie heroes strive to save others, they also seek redemption for themselves. Such was the case in the Disney film *The Finest Hours.*

Actor Christopher Pine plays Captain Bernie Webber of the United States Coast Guard. Quiet, shy, and indecisive, he feels safest when following the rules. When Bernie and his crew fail to save the life of a local fisherman, he is indirectly blamed. Bernie questions his ability and bears the guilt and stigma of failure.

One stormy night, Bernie gets an opportunity to prove himself, and what follows is one of the greatest rescues in the history of the US Coast Guard. To achieve this daunting feat, he has to repeatedly break rules and

---

[88] Brian Godawa, *Hollywood Worldviews* (InterVarsity Press, 2002), 15.

regulations. As the tiny vessel returns safely to the harbor, thirty-two men's lives are saved. Bernie overcomes his personal flaws, his life is redeemed, and his insecurities are replaced with confidence. He is forgiven by those who bore him a grudge, accepted by his peers, and hailed as a hero. And, of course, he gets the girl and they live happily ever after.

Even Superman is a flawed hero. Time and time again, he struggles with moral dilemmas while being confronted with foes whose powers equal or exceed his own. He ages. Kryptonite renders him as weak as a little child. And in the end, he is killed fighting a creature called Doomsday.

Godawa observes, "The story of Superman is a classic American tale that many say embodies the mythical retelling of the life of Christ."[89] I agree. However, Superman is not Christ, for Christ is without limitation or weakness. Since Superman is a product of the human imagination, he is shackled with human limitations and imperfections.

Godawa also observes, "The spiritual aspect of these abilities has been secularized, reinterpreted through evolutionary myth as the result of mutation, the metaphor remains the same."[90]

The story changes, but it always points to the struggle against evil and the redemptive hope of salvation.

The great Francis Schaeffer pointed out that the gods of Greece and Rome were merely "amplified humanity, not divinity."[91] The heroes of antiquity, like Hollywood's superheroes of today, are only shadows of something greater, clues pointing to the divine hero of the "One Story."

All heroes of the human imagination are flawed, just like the rest of us. For this reason, the redemption they offer does not last and is not ultimately satisfying. Superman must save the world again and again. Likewise, our inner problems, fears, and sins must be addressed repeatedly. Though we win the occasional battle, the war to overcome our flaws rages on with each new personal failure or mistake so we continue to struggle. Who will save us from this terrible dilemma?

The salvation we long for finds its perfect expression in the hero of the "One Story." Christ is the hero the world is searching for, whether they realize it or not. He is the romantic partner people long for. He is the only

---

[89] Godawa, 28–29.
[90] Godawa, 28.
[91] Francis Schaeffer, *How Should We Then Live?* (Westchester, IL: Crossway, 1982), 85.

one who can heal us completely and give us lasting peace, love, and the promise of a future beyond death.

Because Jesus was a man and deity, he alone can offer us a redemption that is satisfying and complete. Unlike the heroes of our imagination, Christ's power is without limit. Jesus said,

> Do not be afraid. I am the First and the Last. I am the Living One; I was dead and behold I am alive forevermore.[92]

> Come to me, all you who are weary and burdened, and I will give you rest.[93]

> I am the way the truth and the life. No one comes to the Father except through me.[94]

> For God so loved the world that he gave his one and only Son that whosoever believes in him shall not perish but have eternal life.[95]

How do we approach this one true hero and secure the redemption we seek? Consider the two criminals who were crucified with Jesus. Luke's gospel says,

> One of the criminals who hung there hurled insults at him: "Aren't you the Christ? Save yourself and us!"

> But the other criminal rebuked him. "Don't you fear God," he said, "since you are under the same sentence? We are punished justly, for we are getting what our deeds deserve. But this man has done nothing wrong." Then he said, "Jesus, remember me when you come into your kingdom."

---

[92] Revelation 1:17–18.
[93] Matthew 11:28.
[94] John 14:6.
[95] John 3:16.

Jesus answered him, "I tell you the truth, today you will be with me in paradise."[96]

The first man mocked Jesus, and there is nothing in scripture that indicates any remorse or repentance on his part. He died as he lived: in frustration and rebellion, blaming others for his flaws, and cursing the darkness.

The other man defended Jesus. Admitting his guilt and confessing his sinfulness, he opened the door to God's redemption. John wrote, "If we confess our sins, he is faithful and just and will forgive our sins and purify us from all unrighteousness."[97]

The second man believed that Jesus was the Messiah, the Son of the living God. He did not expect Jesus to step down off the cross, spare his life, and save the day. Had that been his intent, Jesus would not have responded as he did. The thief was seeking redemption not for his physical life but for his soul. He was looking for forgiveness, which Jesus provided.

The second man in the story reached out to the one true hero. And he found salvation that day. He was redeemed because he yielded his life to the one who would yield his life for us all. Like King Theoden and Bernie Webber, the thief found his way home that day. Though his physical life was forfeit, he knew peace and joy as he passed from this life to the next, for his soul was in the hands of the one hero who said, "I am the way the truth and the life. No one comes to the Father except through me."[98]

To do as that thief did, and as I have done, you need only pray in sincerity to Jesus, asking him to forgive your sins and to take your life and make it new. He will.

But be patient with the process, because true change takes time. Find a Bible-believing church where you can meet other believers, commit to following Jesus to the best of your ability, and you will grow in your newfound faith.

This is the victory that was accomplished by Christ's first coming into the world: the opportunity for a personal redemption to anyone who reaches out to him.

---

[96] Luke 23:39–43.
[97] 1 John 1:9.
[98] John 14:6.

Now we will turn our attention to global redemption and restoration of this world, Christ's return: his Second Coming. Jesus said to his apostles before he ascended into heaven, "I am going to prepare a place for you. And if I go and prepare a place for you, I will come back and take you to be with me that you may be where I am."[99] Christ the hero will return to defeat and destroy evil once and for all and to redeem his creation from the curse of death and decay, marking the end to the "One Story."

There is considerable disagreement among Christian scholars as to the exact sequence of events and their symbolism, not to mention the prophecies of the "end times" referred to in the book of Revelation. I will not be investing any time in the minutiae of such theological details but will focus exclusively on the key components of the biblical information concerning the return of Christ and the establishment of his earthly kingdom.

The closing pages of the Bible offer a prophetic picture of the final chapters of human history. They tell of a growing darkness, a final conflict, the return of the King, and his ultimate victory over evil. It is the final eucatastrophe, the conclusion to the "One Story."

The tale is told by John the apostle, who saw a vision from God. John's Revelation is an overview and summation of the story of the conflict between good and evil and the end of the curse of decay and death. The account takes the form of a letter that was circulated among the major churches of Asia decades after Christ's crucifixion. During this time, churches suffered under the extreme and constant persecution of Rome. The letter encouraged believers, giving them hope in face of a foe that could not be defeated by strength of arms. Revelation offers this same hope to present-day believers who face the dilemma of a declining church and a world filled with dark realities that defy solution.

The book of Revelation points to these realities using the symbolism of the "four riders of the apocalypse." Some people mistakenly assume these "riders" will be released at end of time to wreak havoc on our world as part of God's punishment. But according to Edward A. McDowell, author of *The Meaning and Message of the Book of Revelation,* these riders

---

[99] John 14:2–3.

are of our own making and not God's at all. And they have been part of human history from the very beginning.

> The four horsemen represent Conquest, War, Famine, and Death, in this order. These have been the scourges of humankind from early history. They appear and reappear in history in the order in which they appear in John's vision. The author's arrangement is thus a logical one. An individual appears in history, who is fired by ambition to conquer; he must implement his conquest by war; war inevitably brings famine, and the issue of famine is death.[100]

The Romans tried to bring order to our world by means of conquest. They failed. Many others who followed them and preceded them also tried and failed in like manner.

Of all the world's evils, war seems to be the inevitable consequence of our cumulative sin against one another and against God, who fashioned us.

Consider the many appetites that drive us as human beings. Our lust for wealth, power, and pleasure overwhelm our better natures, and we sin not only against one another but also against ourselves. Man's inhumanity against man is the fuel that feeds the furnaces of war.

Jesus's primary teaching was that "man should love God and his neighbor as himself."[101] Instead we love ourselves and pursue our individual appetites, to the ruin of all. According to the scriptures, this pattern of sin, selfishness, and self-destruction will continue as the world moves further away from God. This is the self-imposed curse of sin, the curse that started with Adam and Eve.

When speaking of the end times, Jesus said, "As it was in the days of Noah, so it will be at the coming of the Son of Man."[102] Moses recorded the mindset of Noah's day. "The Lord saw how great the wickedness of

---

[100] Edward A. McDowell, *The Meaning and Message of the Book of Revelation* (Nashville, TN: Broadman Press, 1951), 88–89.
[101] Mark 12:30–31.
[102] Matthew 24:37.

the human race had become on the earth, and that every inclination of the thoughts of the human heart was only evil all the time."[103]

During this period of moral and spiritual decline, the world will eventually be united, politically and economically, in an effort to address its many problems. Revelation speaks of a world economy, a world religion, and a world leader arising in a time of great affluence, achievement, and wealth. This leader is referred to as "the beast." The economy he rules over is referred to as "Babylon," a city of antiquity synonymous with wealth, sensuality, and power. This modern-day empire will span the globe.

At the height of its power, it will begin to erode from the inside out, following the same pattern as the Romans. This world regime will reflect the same disdain for Christians as did Nero and other Caesars who actively persecuted the early church.

True Christians will refuse to compromise what they believe to be God's truth. They will refuse to comply with the dictates of a secular, relativistic government that sees their faith as problematic. As a result, believers will be perceived as antigovernment malcontents, and the practice of their faith will be considered civil disobedience.

Similar perceptions exist today in certain communist and Muslim states, resulting in the denial of human rights, imprisonment, and even execution for those who follow Christ. For these reasons, according to scripture, Christians will face unprecedented persecution under this world regime. Like the Jews of Europe were targeted by the Nazis and the Ukrainians were targeted by the Soviet Communists, Christians will find themselves in the crosshairs of an enemy too powerful to resist.

It is to this world that Christ will return to exact retribution on those who have rejected his truth and offer redemption to those who've embraced it. In the gathering darkness of a world gone mad, when all seems lost, the hero will return.

John the apostle wrote,

> I saw heaven standing open and there before me was a white horse, whose rider is called Faithful and True. With justice he judges and makes war. His eyes are like a blazing

---

[103] Genesis 6:5.

fire and on his head wore many crowns. The armies of heaven were following him, riding on white horses and dressed in fine linen, white and clean.[104]

In John's vision, Christ is wielding a sword fashioned by the hand of God to strike down and destroy evil. He will come to claim what was always his. He will come to judge and rule. And on his robe will be written, "KING OF KINGS AND LORD OF LORDS."[105]

The powers of the world will not greet the coming of the Son of God with rejoicing or worship but with defiance and war. "Then I saw the beast and the kings of the earth and their armies gathered together to make war against the rider on the horse and his army."[106]

The hero crushes all those who oppose him. The victory is one sided and complete. The curse of death and decay is ended. The prophecy of the seed of the woman crushing the head of the serpent is fulfilled as Satan is defeated. The guilty are punished, the faithful are rewarded, and the work of restoring the world begins.

John writes,

> I heard a loud voice from the throne saying, "Now the dwelling of God is with men, and he will live with them and be their God. He will wipe every tear from their eyes. There will be no more death or mourning or crying or pain, for the old order of things has passed away." He who was seated on the throne said, "I am making everything new!"[107]

The remaining words of Revelation describe the healing of the physical world and its scarred environment. Eden is restored to its original splendor. There, amid lush, green land, a beautiful city will be built, bathed in a brilliant light that emanates not from the sun but from God himself. In

---

[104] Revelation 19:11, 12, 14.
[105] Revelation 19:16.
[106] Revelation 19:19.
[107] Revelation 21:3–4.

this new order, the present natural order of time, decay, and death will be discarded in favor of something decidedly better.

The prophet Isaiah writes,

> The wolf will live with the lamb, the leopard will lie down with the goat, the calf and the lion and the yearling together; and the little child will lead them. The cow will feed with the bear, their young will lie down together; the lion will eat straw like the ox. The infant will play near the hole of the cobra, and young child will put his hand into the viper's nest. They will neither harm nor destroy on all my holy mountain, for the earth will be full of the knowledge of the Lord as the waters cover the sea.[108]

As it was in Eden, man and animal will live together in a perfect world nourished by vegetation and fruit. They will breathe clean air and drink clean water, for all things will be as they were in the beginning.

Paul the apostle, in his letter to the Romans, declared that the physical creation looks forward to this day of healing and restoration. "The creation waits in eager expectation for the sons of God to be revealed, that the creation itself will be liberated from its bondage to decay and brought into the glorious freedom of the children of God."[109]

On this great day, all people of the world will rejoice for what God has done through the hero, his Son, Jesus the Christ. This day will mark the end of evil and the dawn of the kingdom of God on earth.

The prophet Malachi wrote,

> Surely the day is coming; it will burn like a furnace. All the arrogant and every evildoer will be stubble, and the day that is coming will set them on fire, says the Lord Almighty. Not a root or a branch will be left to them. But for you who revere my name, the sun of righteousness will rise with healing in its wings. And you will go out and leap like calves released from the stall. Then you will

---

[108] Isaiah 11:6–9.
[109] Romans 8:19, 21.

trample down the wicked; they will be ashes under the soles of your feet on the day when I do these things, says the Lord Almighty.[110]

This will be the happy ending to the "One Story" and the beginning of a new story for all those throughout history who have placed their faith in Christ, the ultimate hero.

Some take offense at the idea of final judgment and justice. Such was the case with Friedrich Nietzsche. Nietzsche detested the idea of Christ the hero, decrying what he believed to be the grave injustice of so-called Christians rejoicing at the demise of their fellow human beings on the day of God's judgment. Seeing Christians as hypocrites, he warned his followers, "We must not let ourselves be led away: 'judge not!' they say, but they dispatch all those to hell who stand in their way."[111] Nietzsche mistook believers' joy for gloating.

When Malachi writes that believers "will leap like calves released from their stalls," he refers to their celebration of freedom from sin and evil, not of the demise of their enemies. Since what has taken place will not be the result of their own power or resolve, why would they gloat over those who sought their destruction? Such an unimaginable and miraculous gift of deliverance should elicit only one logical response: thankfulness.

In *The Return of the King*, when Sam rejoiced over the destruction of the ring and his master being freed from its power, he was not gloating over the destruction of Sauron and his hosts. Sam was rejoicing in the salvation of his master and the people of Middle Earth. "In all the ruin of the world, for the moment he felt only joy, great joy. The burden was gone. His master had been saved: he was himself again, he was free."[112]

Author and philosopher John Davenport observes,

> In this event, we see Tolkien's point that a true eucatastrophe is humbling, and thus precisely the opposite

---

[110] Malachi 4:1–3.

[111] Friedrich Nietzsche, translated by Anthony M. Ludovici, *The Antichrist* (Prometheus Books, 2000), 65.

[112] J. R. R. Tolkien, *The Return of the King* (Houghton Mifflin Company, 2002), 958.

of the vengeful spirit of triumph that Nietzsche saw in the Christian hope of Christ's return and a day of judgment.[113]

The idea that evil must be punished, however distasteful to some, is a universally accepted principle found in the governmental framework of every nation on earth. Its roots are deeply embedded in the human understanding of justice. While none should rejoice in the suffering of other human beings, regardless of how foul their deeds, the need to punish such deeds remains.

The vast majority of people in the world believe that evil must be punished. To neglect to do so would represent a moral and ethical failure. If a crime has been committed that caused the suffering or death of another human being, appropriate punishment and recompense must be meted out. When the legal system of any country fails to administer judgment in response to a crime, people will protest what they rightfully perceive to be a failure to secure justice.

This moral awareness reveals itself in human beings at an early age. Laura E. Berk, professor of psychology and author of the primary textbook for human development, writes,

> Children do not just copy their morality from others. As the cognitive-developmental approach emphasized, they actively think about right and wrong. As early as the age of six, children view freedom of speech and religion as individual rights, even if laws exist to deny those rights (Helwig and Turiel, 2002).[114]

This ability to wrestle with complex moral issues at a young age points to the innate nature of the human passion for justice. The piece of eternity God placed in our hearts cares about what is right and what is wrong. With this understanding comes the necessity for punishment.

Failure to punish the guilty becomes yet another injustice. If a man rapes and murders a twelve-year-old girl, how do civilized people

---

[113] John J. Davenport, *The Lord of the Rings and Philosophy* (Open Court Publishing Company, a division of Carus Publishing Company, 2003), 216.

[114] Laura E. Berk, *Development through the Lifespan* (Pearson Education Inc., 2007), 337–338.

respond? If a woman entrusted with the funds of a charitable organization embezzles half a million dollars, how does society react? What about the horrific acts of genocide perpetrated by the Nazis against the Jews and the Japanese against the Chinese? The world demands that justice be served on those who commit such atrocities. To fail to judge and punish in such cases would be considered by most people as immoral as the crimes themselves.

The biblical notion of a day of judgment is no different from the judgments we place on one another for comparable offenses. What kind of God would fail to do what a reasonably competent public official does on a regular basis? If the "One Story" is to end happily, evil must be vanquished and punished, securing justice and equity for all. Christ will accomplish this Herculean feat, bringing light and peace and justice, and a world made perfect and new, for all those who place their faith in him. This is the hope of the "One Story." It is also the hope of the Christian: the hope of a world restored, a perfect world with God at the head.

To some, this is nothing more than a fool's hope, which finds its roots in the unrealistic idealism of adolescent and immature minds. Psychologist Laura Berk observed,

> Adolescents' capacity to think about possibilities opens up the world of the ideal and of perfection. Teenagers imagine alternative family, religious, political and moral systems, and they want to explore them. As a result they often construct grand visions (stories) of a perfect world with no injustice, discrimination or tasteless behavior.[115]

Are these the musings of naive adolescents or the manifestation of truth itself residing in the deepest recesses of the human heart and mind, placed there by the hand of God? Author A. D. Jameson touches on the idea of a more perfect world in his book *I Find Your Lack of Faith Disturbing: Star Wars and the Triumph of the Geek Culture*. He challenges the notion that superhero films and other fantasies are merely escapism.

---

[115] Berk, 385.

"It's an old prejudice: geeks are immature losers who can't hack it in the real world."[116]

He goes on to reference this prejudice as a common stereotype. "Geeks would rather retreat to made-up, simpler places, safe places, inhabited by imaginary friends, than deal with the hard complexities of the actual world."[117] Atheists view Christians in much the same sense. Jameson, however, sees something positive in fantasy and the hope of a better world.

> *Star Trek* was more than just a T.V. show, *X-Men* more than just a comic. They were my means of dreaming of a better life, and I invested a great deal of myself in them from the age of ten through eighteen. I am not embarrassed to admit I'd rather live in the world that *Star Trek* depicts, in terms of morals and freedom from scarcity, than the world I currently live in, and that isn't just escapism—its aspiration.[118]

It is not strange that people hope for a better world than the one they know. Hundreds of millions of moviegoers prove that point year after year. The people who attend Comic-Con are not alone in their desire for a better world or, as Jameson puts it, "some stable other world."[119] The majority of humankind secretly longs for a perfect world, whether they recognize it or not. The same hope resides in the hearts and minds of all the great storytellers who, despite life's harsh realities, continue to look for justice, joy, and peace.

Tolkien wrote of the makers of legend in his poem "Mythopeia."

> These storytellers are blessed as they speak of things outside of recorded time: though they have looked at death and even ultimate defeat, they have not flinched and retreated in despair. Instead, they have often sung of

---

[116] A. D. Jameson, *I Find Your Lack of Faith Disturbing: Star Wars and the Triumph of the Geek Culture* (Farrar, Straus and Giroux, 2018), 210.
[117] Jameson, 211.
[118] Jameson, 214–215.
[119] Jameson, 228.

victory, and the fire in their voices, caught from legend, has kindled the hearts of their listeners. In so doing, they have lit up both the darkness of the past and the present day with the brightness of suns, as yet by no man seen.[120]

This is the brightness of hope that the teller of the "One Story" offers. It is not a fool's hope but a genuine one—a hope that nothing in this life can extinguish or even lessen for those who believe. A hope that the happy ending we all search for is more than just the fanciful wish of the very young and the very old, but that it is absolute truth.

---

[120] Colin Duriez, *Tolkien and C. S. Lewis: The Gift of Friendship* (Hidden Spring, an imprint of Paulist Press, 2003), 179.

CHAPTER EIGHT

WHAT DOES YOUR HEART TELL YOU?

In director George Seaton's holiday movie *Miracle on 34th Street,* an idealistic lawyer named Fred attempts to prove in a court of law that Santa Claus exists. At the same time, he is also trying to convince his skeptical fiancée, Doris, that Macy's department store Santa, a Mr. Kris Kringle, is that person.

In the pivotal scene of that film, we find the couple arguing the point. Having given up his position at a prestigious law firm to defend Kris, the young lawyer attempts to explain why he is doing it to his confused and annoyed fiancée, who views the effort as a waste of time. As the argument escalates, he implores Doris to have faith him while she insists that he exercise common sense and drop the case.

The young lawyer argues that life's intangibles—things like love, faith, joy, and hope—are some of the important ideas that Santa represents. His fiancée, however, is more concerned with the realities of life, like a good job and the paycheck that goes along with it.

The argument concludes when Fred blurts out,

> Look, Doris, someday you are going to find out that your
> way of facing this realistic world just doesn't work and

when you do, don't overlook those lovely intangibles. You'll discover they are the only things that are worthwhile![121]

The young lawyer was right. In the end, intangible things outweigh everything else because they are the things we need most in life.

Of all the intangibles that define the complex combination of attributes, behaviors, and thoughts that make us human, perhaps none is more potent or more mysterious than humankind's universal need for hope. Hope is at the center of the "One Story."

My qualifications for speaking about hope are twofold: first and foremost, I am a believer whose hope is in Christ; second, I am a fisherman. Few people in this world understand hope better than someone who fishes.

My son and I have spent considerable time fishing over the years. Whether we caught a great many fish or none at all, just before it's time to head home, one of us will say, "Just one more cast." Which actually means anywhere from three to six casts. The hope of catching just one more fish drives us.

In his book *Pavlov's Trout,* Paul Quinnett points out that we can learn something about Christian hope from fishermen. He writes,

> It is better to fish hopefully than to catch fish. Fishing is hope experienced. To be optimistic in a slow bite is to thrive on hope alone. When asked, "How can you fish all day without a hit?" the true fisherman replies, "Hold it! I think I felt something." If the line goes slack, he says "He'll be back!" When it comes to the human spirit, hope is all. Without hope, there is no yearning, no desire for a better tomorrow, and no belief that the next cast will bring the big strike. According to scripture, the Christian life is "hope experienced," and a hopeless Christian is a contradiction in terms.[122]

---

[121] *Miracle on 34th Street,* directed by George Seaton (Twentieth Century Fox, 1947).
[122] Paul Quinnett, *Pavlov's Trout: The Incomplete Psychology of Everyday Fishing* (Keokee Co. Publishing, 2012), 210.

Not all people share in the light that hope provides. The world is filled with hopeless people who are overwhelmed by misfortune or dire circumstance. Others see hope as nothing more than a self-induced delusion. Aristotle called hope "a waking dream."[123] Benjamin Franklin said, "He that lives upon hope will die fasting."[124] Voltaire said, "Hope should no more be a virtue than 'fear'; we fear and we hope, according to what is promised or threatened us."[125] Nietzsche wrote, "Hope in reality is worst of all evils, because it prolongs the torments of man."[126] For Voltaire, hope was simply an emotion like fear—irrational and oftentimes pointless.

For Nietzsche, the quintessential atheist, hope was evil so an illusion best forsaken. He would recommend that we accept the meaninglessness of life, do as we please, embrace the darkness, and die. Strangely enough, this is often what people do when hope is forsaken or lost.

In his book *Man's Search for Meaning*, Viktor Frankl tells of his years trapped in the indescribable horror of German concentration camps at Auschwitz and Dachau. He was transported there like a despised animal and given two minutes to strip naked or be whipped. Every hair was shaved from his body, and he was condemned to a living death. His father, mother, brother, and wife died in the camps or were sent to the gas ovens. His existence was full of cold, fear, starvation, pain, lice and vermin, dehumanization, exhaustion, and terror. Frankl wrote that he was able to survive because he never lost the quality of hope.

Those prisoners who lost faith in the future were doomed. When a prisoner lost hope, Frankl said, he let himself decline, becoming subject to mental and physical decay. He would die from the inside out. Frankl said that this usually happened quite suddenly. One morning a prisoner would just refuse to get up. He wouldn't get dressed, wash, or go outside to the parade grounds. No amount of pleading by his fellow prisoners would help. No threatening by the captors would have any effect. Having lost all hope, he had simply given up. He would lie there in his own excrement until he died.

---

[123] Aristotle, quoted by translator R. D. Hickin Diogenes Laertius's *Live and Opinions of Eminent Philosophers* (third-century AD).

[124] Benjamin Franklin, *The Way to Wealth* (July 7, 1757).

[125] Voltaire, *Virtue* (Philosophical Dictionary, 1764).

[126] Nietzsche, *Human, All Too Human*, translated by Helen Zimmern (1878), 71.

American soldiers later told Frankl this behavior pattern also existed among prisoners of war and was called "give-up-itis." When a prisoner lost hope, said Frankl, "he lost his spiritual hold."[127]

Nietzsche was right in one respect when he said, "Hope in reality is the worst of all evils."[128] His personal hope was placed in man, and in the course of time man destroyed what little hope Nietzsche possessed. Hope is often misplaced in things like power, wealth, and political or philosophical ideas, all of which ultimately fail, leaving those who trusted in them disillusioned and confused.

Without hope, something in a human being dies.

Author John Maxwell talks about a small town in Maine that was proposed for the site of a great hydroelectric plant. A dam would be built across the river and the town submerged.

> When the project was announced, the people were given many months to arrange their affairs and relocate. During those months, a curious thing happened. All improvements ceased. No painting was done. No repairs were made on the buildings, roads, or sidewalks. Day by day the whole town got shabbier. A long time before the waters came, the town looked uncared for and abandoned, even though the people had not yet moved away. One citizen explained: "Where there is no faith in the future, there is no power in the present." The town was cursed with hopelessness because it had no future.[129]

The "One Story" sets before us a hope with a future, a hope that reaches beyond the boundaries of this existence to another life and another world.

Author Thornton Wilder wrote,

[127] Victor E. Frankl, *Man's Search for Meaning* (New York: Washington Square Press, 1984), 95, 163.
[128] Nietzsche, *Human, All Too Human*, translated by Helen Zimmern (1878), 71.
[129] John Maxwell, *Your Attitude* (San Bernardino, CA: Here's Life Publishers, 1984), 120.

Hope is a projection of the imagination; so is despair. Despair all too readily embraces the ills it foresees; hope is the energy that arouses the mind to explore every possibility to combat them. In response to hope the imagination is aroused to picture every possible issue and to try every door.[130]

Hope moves us ever forward while hopelessness will stop us dead in our tracks.

In his book *Wining Life's Battles,* psychologist Julius Segal wrote about the 25,000 American soldiers who were held by the Japanese in POW camps during World War II.

Forced to exist under inhumane conditions, many of them died. Others, however, survived and eventually returned home. There was no reason to believe there was any difference in the stamina of these two groups of soldiers. The survivors, however, were different in one major respect: They confidently expected to be released someday (they hoped). They talked about the kinds of homes they would have, the jobs they would choose, and even described the kind of person they would marry. They drew pictures on the walls to illustrate their dreams. Some even found ways to study subjects related to the kind of career they wanted to pursue.[131]

Hope separated many of those who survived from those who did not. Hope motivated them to some kind of action.

Tolkien spoke of hope in his essay *On Fairy-Stories.* He argued that stories of fantasy could instill genuine hope in a person whose life might otherwise seem hopeless, just like those American prisoners who fantasized about what their lives could be in the future. Tolkien wrote,

---

[130] Thornton Wilde, *Theophilus North* (Avon Books, A division of Hearst Corporation, 1973), 275, 334.
[131] Dr. Julius Segal, *Winning Life's Toughest Battles* (New York: Ivy Books, 1996), 95–97.

Why should a man be scorned, if, finding himself in prison, he tries to get out and go home? Or if, when he can't do so, he thinks and talks about other topics than jailers or prison walls? The world outside has not become less real because the prisoner cannot see it.[132]

Emily Dickinson said, "Hope is a strange invention, a Patent of the Heart in unremitting action, yet never wearing out."[133] Hope sustains our lives and dreams. It is the most needed of all of life's intangibles.

The Bible has much to say on the subject of hope. Paul wrote to the Romans, "Everything that was written in the past was written to teach us, so that through the scriptures we might have hope."[134]

Hope enables us to believe in things like love, joy, peace, and truth. Carl Sandburg said, "Hope is an echo, hope ties itself yonder, yonder."[135] Hope comes from heaven, echoing in humankind's collective heart the unmistakable and inexplicable truth that we are more than just animals and that life is more than it seems.

C. S. Lewis said, "Hope is a continual looking forward to the eternal world."[136] There is an unmistakably divine aspect to hope for which the world has no explanation.

Author Charles Allen, in his book *The Miracle of Love,* endeavors to describe part of this mystery when he writes,

G. F. Watt has a famous painting entitled *Hope.* It pictures a poor woman against the world. Her eyes are bandaged so that she cannot see ahead. In her hands is a harp, but all the strings are broken save one. Those broken strings represent her shattered expectations and her bitter disappointments. The one last unbroken string is the string of hope. She strikes that string and a glorious melody floats out over the world and it fills her dark skies with stars. The artist

---

[132] Verlyn Flieger, *Tolkienon Fairy-Stories* (HarperCollins UK, 2014).
[133] Emily Dickinson, poem (c. 1877).
[134] Romans 15:4.
[135] Carl Sandburg, *The People, Yes* (1936).
[136] C. S. Lewis, *The Joyful Christian* (Macmillan Publishing Co., 1977), 138.

painted a great truth: Even when all else is gone, you still have hope.[137]

Poet Emily Dickinson recognized the melody to which Watt pointed and set it to rhyme.

Hope is the thing with feathers
That perches in the soul,
And sings the tune without words,
And never stops at all.[138]

Hope is a beautiful, powerful, and mysterious thing that people need to survive the difficulties and challenges of life. Its echo is that of a song we once knew but have, over the course of time, forgotten and can no longer recognize or even hear.

A wise old priest named Joseph Roux said, "At first we hope too much, later on, not enough."[139] As children, we believed everything, so our hopes were boundless. As adults, we learn to believe in little and hope in even less. As children, we heard the music of hope. But with the passing of years, with its many disappointments, difficulties, and losses, we forget the melody. As children, we believed; as adults, we only doubt. We have lost something precious.

To summarize my thoughts, I would like to share with you the story of a little boy who grew up to be a wonderful young man who did not forget the melody of hope or the song it sings. His story is one of heroes, light, and hope.

In his book *Life Animated,* Pulitzer Prize-winning author Ron Suskind tells the story of his youngest son, Owen. At the age of three, symptoms of autism surfaced. The child withdrew into his own world. The family did everything they could to aid Owen in his struggle. They enlisted help from doctors, teachers, and specialists. Those who worked with the Suskinds provided tremendous help in Owen's progress. However, according to

---

[137] Charles L. Allen, *The Miracle of Love* (Old Tappan, NJ: Fleming H. Revell Co., 1972), 71.

[138] Emily Dickinson, "Hope Is the Thing with Feathers," in *A Treasury of Poems,* compiled by Sarah Anne Stuart (BBS Publishing Corporation, 1996), 273.

[139] Joseph Roux, *Meditations of a Parish Priest,* translated by Isabel F. Hapgood (1886), 5–8.

Suskind, Owen's inexplicable connection with certain Disney animated films was what finally moved him out of autism's imposed darkness and back into the light of day.

After a prolonged period of silence, Owen began communicating by using words, phrases, and sentences from *The Little Mermaid, The Jungle Book, Aladdin,* and *The Lion King,* films that Owen had enjoyed watching with his older brother, Walt, and his mother and father, before the onset of the autistic behavior.

As evidence mounted concerning the Disney phenomenon, the Suskinds decided to visit "the happiest place on earth." The results were nothing short of "magical."

> It is as if nothing has changed, as if the last year and a half was a bad dream. By mid-afternoon it's clear that Owen isn't self-talking in the streams of gibberish, or flapping his hands as he usually does. Some, but not much. He seems calm and focused. Owen seems at home here, as though his identity—or however much of it has formed— is somehow tied to this place.[140]

On a second trip to Disney World a few years later, Owen exhibited the same settled pattern of behavior. Ron observed,

> He is expressive and affectionate with these characters in ways he rarely is with us, or anyone else. Cornelia and I talk about this in the café at the Wilderness Lodge that night. Is it okay for him to have such a strong emotional bond with them? Is there a danger here? Are there views and truths he was ingesting that were all but invisible to our adult eyes?[141]

Viewing the Disney theme parks as an artificial world, the Suskinds grappled with the moral dilemma of whether they were indirectly

[140] Ron Suskind, *Life Animated: A Story of Sidekicks, Heroes, and Autism* (Glendale, CA: Kingswell, an imprint of Disney Publishing Worldwide, 2014), 28.
[141] Suskind, 73.

contributing to their son's confusion by bringing him to such a place. Wouldn't it be better if he embraced reality? What truths or views would such an artificial experience teach their son about the life that lay before him?

Perhaps part of the answer lies in Tolkien's belief that fantasy offers "a sudden glimpse of the underlying reality of truth." Myth and truth can be one and the same. The stories of fantasy can teach us things that will help us face the harsh realities of life.

As the Suskinds continued their discussion, both Ron and Cornelia conceded that when Owen was at Disney World, he was

> more attentive, affectionate, and available to us ... even if, after seventy-two hours neck deep in Disney artifice, we can't wait to get back to the real world. Owen could stay here forever. He is comfortable at home and he's comfortable here.[142]

I believe what the Suskinds were discovering about Disney's fantasy world is what Tolkien was making reference to concerning the power of myth. As their son consumed what was being offered in this artificial place, he utilized it as a source of empowerment to deal with his own reality.

Another part of Owen's story that fascinated me was the divine aspect of his experience. His mother is a Christian and his father is Jewish, so the idea of God was very much welcome in their home.

Suskind observed that on more than one occasion, Owen demonstrated an almost inexplicable ability to pray, not only constructing whole sentences but also demonstrating a cognitive understanding of fairly complex ideas. Recalling a St. Patrick's Day dinner following the tragedy of 9/11 and the beginning of the Afghanistan War in March of that same year, Suskind recorded the following incident:

> I turn off the radio as Cornelia and I bring out the big serving dishes of corned beef in its cabbage stew and

---

[142] Suskind, 73–74.

homemade soda bread. She suggests we say grace. We go around the table, each of us offering a bit of something—all now joined hands—until we come to Owen.

"Would you like to say something, honey?"
He looks quizzically, confused it seems about the concept. "It's just talking to God," she says. "That's all."
Owen nods once. He understands.

"Dear God," he says after a moment. "Let the people around the world tonight find peace and honor, freedom, and choice." He stops, looks at each of us. "And may we at this table always be part of one another." On a night when the nation, and much of the world, is gripped with tension—an anxiety we're sure Owen could feel, even if he didn't understand all its particulars—we asked him to say a little something. Maybe what's missing in him, the reasonable doubts and common hesitations, allows him to look upward, unfettered, in a way that focuses some invisible capacities. After all, it's a big deal to talk to God, if you believe he can actually hear you. All of this I think about, walking the floors as dawn approaches, wondering how it's possible, after all of our efforts, that just about the most cogent and heartfelt thing my son has ever uttered was to a deity I didn't much believe in.[143]

I would agree with Suskind that maybe Owen's malady freed him from the distractions of this existence to better comprehend the reality of another. Could it be that in a world that seldom makes sense, particularly during a time of war, the idea of a God who can help us would make perfect sense not only to Owen but to us all? Certainly Suskind was wrestling with one of life's intangibles as he tried to make sense out of Owen's prayer to a deity he wasn't really sure he believed in.

---

[143] Suskind, 109.

At Owen's bar mitzvah, it happened again. Having negotiated the reading of his section of the Torah in Hebrew successfully, he was afforded the opportunity to give a speech. His talk focused on loving God and your neighbor as yourself. I have been a pastor for close to forty years, and I have never heard a preacher or a theologian explain the concept of *love thy neighbor* better than Owen did. Suskind, reflecting on his Jewish heritage and Owen's closing thoughts, noted,

> A handful who remember he ended his speech with "My prayers always start with the word *hope*" tend to come from my side, who know that the word *hatikva* means *hope* in Hebrew. That's the song—the Israeli national anthem—he then played on the piano to finish the service.[144]

I believe enlightenment and, more importantly, hope were what Owen found in Disney's repeated versions of the "One Story." Hope not only for his own circumstances but hope for his loved ones struggling with cancer, hope in the face of tragedy and even war, and hope for all people and for the world. I believe that the inexplicable events of Owen's life point to the power of the stories he loves. Like me, Owen found in those stories faith, hope, love, a happy ending, and a future to look forward to.

Owen's story reveals the experiences of many who have found something intangible yet very real in the "One Story." For Owen, it was a personal kind of salvation that empowered him to accept himself as he was, autism and all, and in his words to be "OK" with that. For others, it is the triumph of light over darkness; for still others, the hope of justice and equity for all. In the final analysis, in whatever form it takes in the mind of an individual, people find *hope* in the "One Story."

Many people see the Walt Disney Company as nothing more than a marketing enterprise. But historically, Disney has been infinitely more. The vastness of their reach and their effectiveness in capturing and holding our attention, along with their seemingly endless ability to touch minds and hearts, lies in the fact that they are marketers of *hope*. In movie after movie, they tell of light's triumph over darkness and finding love and a

---

[144] Suskind, 132–133.

happy ending. They answer the call of our hearts and give us hope that the good things we most desire to see and experience are possible, if not in this life then in the next. Fantasy brings all these possibilities to life.

For the Christian, hope is more than just the story of a babe born in Bethlehem or the story of the crucified and risen Christ. Our story is not yet complete. We live in hope of the hero's return, the destruction of evil, the healing of this world, and the happy ending only God can provide. Without such a hope, life loses all meaning and the song that would otherwise fill the human heart goes silent and dies.

Such was the case with Charles Darwin, who abandoned the idea of the Christian God as a myth, forsaking his belief in God in favor of his vast intellect. Following this decision, Darwin articulated the loss of something he didn't fully understand.

> Up to the age of thirty or beyond it, poetry of many kinds ... gave me great pleasure, and even as a school boy I took intense delight in Shakespeare ... Formerly pictures gave me considerable, and very great delight. But now for many years I cannot endure to read a line of poetry: I have tried to read Shakespeare, and found it so intolerably dull that it nauseated me. I have also almost lost any taste for pictures or music ... I retain some taste for fine scenery, but it does not cause me the exquisite delight which if formerly did ... My mind seems to have become a kind of machine for grinding general laws out of large collections of facts ... The loss of these tastes is a loss of happiness, and may possibly be injurious to the intellect, and more probably to the moral character, by enfeebling the emotional part of our nature.[145]

What Darwin explained as "the loss of these tastes" was the loss of hope. Without God, the mystery of creation and life itself was transformed into nothing more than protoplasm and inarticulate matter. What was once beautiful was reduced to mere facts and figures. What was once

---

[145] Philip Yancey, *Rumors of Another World* (Michigan: Zondervan, 2003), 23.

awe-inspiring became meaningless. There was no song, no story, and no hope.

Author and apologist G. K. Chesterton observed, "The madman is not the man who has lost his reason. The madman is the man who has lost everything except his reason."[146]

Albert Einstein wrote,

> The most beautiful thing we can experience is the mysterious. It is the source of all true art and science. He to whom this emotion is a stranger, who can no longer pause to wonder and stand rapt in awe, is as good as dead: his eyes are closed.[147]

Einstein believed in God. He hoped for something more than his physical eyes could see, and this hope gave him joy as a person and focus as a scientist.

What do you hope for? What does your heart tell you? When you look at the stars, marvel at a sunset or sunrise, stand on the beach, and gaze at the vastness of the ocean, what do you see? Who do you hear? Solomon said that God placed eternity in the hearts of men yet they cannot fathom what he has done from the beginning to the end. Theologian Rudolf Otto described this phenomenon when he wrote, "It might best be understood as seeing this present life as haunted by something that, although invisible, is nevertheless a real presence."[148]

The "One Story," like so many of life's intangibles, points directly to the "real presence" of which Otto spoke: the Christian God. I believe that the "One Story" and humankind's inexplicable fascination with it is a clue pointing to the one true God, who first revealed himself to the ancient Hebrews and then to the world through the efforts of the Christians who followed them.

To Einstein, it was a mystery. To Tolkien, a story. To C. S. Lewis, a longing. To Otto, the haunting presence of something moving unseen in the world. To Owen, a light in the darkness. To men and women grappling

---

[146] G. K. Chesterton, *Orthodoxy* (San Francisco: Ignatius Press, 1995), 24.

[147] Albert Einstein, essay, *Living Philosophies* (Simon & Schuster, 1931).

[148] Barry Morrow, *Heaven Observed* (Colorado Springs: NavPress, 2001), 106.

with life's many trials, the hope of something better. To the poor, weary, downtrodden, and oppressed, it is a vision of final justice and equity. For those who grieve man's violation of God's creation in nature, it is the hope that one day our world will be healed and restored to its original perfection. For all those who place their faith in the one true God and his Son, Jesus the Christ, the "One Story" means a happy ending in heaven and a world made new.

The stories we create and recreate over and over again look for the same hero, the same love, and the same redemption. The question is and always will be "Why do we care about this story?" There are only two possible answers. The "One Story" means nothing, as Campbell thought, or it is the central truth to all existence and the only true hope we have as human beings.

In this modest work, I have only scratched the surface of a matter too deep and complex to be fully understood or articulated by one individual. My desire was simply to raise the question, believing that others more insightful than me might build upon the foundation of this idea.

To believe in the message of the "One Story" is to hope in the mystery of the unseen, believing that eventually it will become a reality. This is my hope for you who read these words: that you will find in Jesus the happy ending your heart has for so long sought. Jesus said, "For God so loved the world that he gave his one only Son, that whosoever believes in him, shall not perish but have eternal life."[149] This is good news for us all, and without a doubt, it is the beginning and the end to the most wonderful story ever told, for those who embrace it will indeed live happily ever after.

---

[149] John 3:16.

BIBLIOGRAPHY

Allen, Charles L. *The Miracle of Love.* Old Tappan, NJ: Fleming H. Revell Co., 1972.

Berk, Laura E. *Development Through the Lifespan.* Pearson Education Inc., 2007.

Campbell, Joseph. *A Hero with a Thousand Faces.* Princeton, New Jersey:Princeton UniversityPress, 1949.

Chesterton, G. K. *Orthodoxy.* San Francisco:Ignatius Press, 1995.

Cotterell, Arthur and RachelStorm. *The Ultimate Encyclopedia ofMythology.* Hermes House,Anness Publishing Ltd., 1999.

Davenport, John J. *The Lord of the Rings and Philosophy.*Open Court Publishing Company, a division of Carus Publishing Company, 2003.

Dickinson, Emily. "Hope Is the Thing with Feathers,"in *A Treasury of Poems,* compiled by SarahAnne Stuart. BBS Publishing Corporation, 1996.

Duriez, Colin. *Tolkien and C. S. Lewis: The Gift of Friendship,* Hidden Spring, an imprint of Paulist Press, 2003.

Ehrlich, Eugene and DeBruhl, Marshall. *The International Thesaurus of Quotations.* HarperCollins, 1996.

Eldredge, John. *Epic.* Nashville, TN:Thomas Nelson, Inc., 2004.

Clifton Fadiman. Edited *Living Philosophies, The Reflections of Some Eminent Men and Women of our Time,* Doubleday Publishing a division of Bantam Doubleday Dell Publishing Group Inc. 1990, quoting Albert Einstein from *Living Philosophies,* Simon and Schuster, 1931

Flieger,Verlyn.*Tolkienon Fairy-Stories.* HarperCollins UK, 2014.

Flowers, Betty Sue, ed., Joseph Campbell, and Bill Moyers, *The Power of Myth.* New York, NY: MJF Books, Fine Communications, 1988.

Frankl, Victor E. *Man's Search for Meaning.* New York: Washington Square Press, 1984.

Gabler, Neal. *Life the Movie.* New York:Vintage Books, adivision of Random House, Inc., 1998.

Glaspey, Terry. *The Spiritual Legacy of C. S. Lewis.* Nashville: CumberlandHouse, 1996.

Godawa, Brian, *Hollywood Worldview.*Downers Grove, IL:Intervarsity Press, 2002.

Gottschall, Jonathan. *The Storytelling Animal.* First Mariner Books, 2013.

Harari, Yuval Noah.*Sapiens: A Brief History of Humankind.*Harper, an imprint ofHarperCollins Publishers, 2015.

Jameson, A.D. *I* Find *Your Lack of Faith Disturbing, Star Wars and The Triumph of the Geek Culture.* Farrar, Straus and Giroux, 2018

Kagan, Neil. *National Geographic Concise History of the World.*The National Geographic Society, 2013.

Kidner, Derek. *Genesis: An Introduction and Commentary.* London, England:The TyndalePress, published in America by InterVarsity Press, 1967.

Lewis, C. S. *The Joyful Christian.* New York:Macmillan Publishing Co., 1977.

Martindale, Walter and JerryRood, eds.*The Quotable Lewis.* Michigan:WilliamB. Eerdmans Publishing Company, 2002.

Maxwell, John. *Your Attitude.* San Bernardino, CA: Here's Life Publishers,1984.

McAllister, Stuart. "Curiosity and Power and Pull of Stories."Lecture notes. Nyack, NY:Alliance Theological Seminary,2004.

McAllister, Stuart."The Rage Against Injustice and Deceit."Lecture notes. Nyack, NY:Alliance Theological Seminary, 2004.

McDowell, Edward A. *The Meaning and Message of the Book of Revelation.* Nashville, TN: Broadman Press, 1951.

Morrow, Barry. *Heaven Observed.* Colorado Springs:NavPress,2001.

Nietzsche, Friedrich. *The Antichrist.*Translated by Anthony M. Ludovici. Amherst, NY:Prometheus Books, 2000.

Quinnett, Paul.*Pavlov's Trout: The Incompleat Psychology of Everyday Fishing.*KeokeeCo. Publishing, 2012.

Richardson, Don. *Eternity in Their Hearts.* Baker Publishing Group, 1981

Segal, Julius. *Winning Life's Toughest Battles.*New York: Ivy Books, 1996.

Smith, Dave. *The Quotable Walt Disney.* New York, NY: Disney Enterprises, Inc., 2001.

Suskind, Ron. *Life Animated: A Story of Sidekicks, Heroes, and Autism* (Glendale, CA:Kingswell, an imprint of Disney Publishing Worldwide, 2014.

Taylor, Daniel. *The Healing Power of Stories: Creating Yourself through the Stories of Your Life.* Dublin: Gill & Macmillan, 1996.

Tolkien, J. R. R.*The Return of the King.* Houghton Mifflin Company, 1955.

Truitt, Brian, quoting J. Michael Staczynski. "A Look Under the Hoodie of Superman."*USA Today,* October 28, 2010.

Unger, Merrill F. *Archaeology and the Old Testament.* Zondervan Publishing House, 1954, 1963.

Webster's II New College Dictionary, Houghton Mifflin Company, 2002.

Patterson, Ben.*The Grand Essentials.* Quoting Thornton Wilde. Word Books, 1989.

Yancey, Philip. *Rumors of Another World.* Michigan: Zondervan, 2003.

CPSIA information can be obtained
at www.ICGtesting.com
Printed in the USA
BVHW081651121022
649303BV00014B/105